DR. MINNIE CLAIBORNE

Prayer
therapy

STOP HURTING!

Copyright © Dr. Minnie Claiborne 2006

All rights reserved. No part of this publication may be produced, distributed, or transmitted in any form or by any means, including photocopying, recording, or other electronic or mechanical methods, without the prior written permision of the publisher, except in the case of brief quotations embodied in critical reviews and certain other noncommercial uses permitted by copyright law.
For permission requests, write to the publisher, addressed "Attention: Permissions Coordinator" at the email address below:

Life and Success Media Ltd
email info@abookinsideyou.com
www.abookinsideyou.com

This publication is designed to provide accurate and authoritative information in regard to the subject matter covered. It is sold with the understanding that the publisher is not engaged in rendering legal, accounting, or other professional service. If legal advice or other expert assistance is required, the services of a competent professional should be sought.

ISBN: 978-1-907402-90-6

Cover design by
www.miadesign.com

CONTENTS

FOREWORD
Natalie Cole

DEDICATION

INTRODUCTION

1	THE DISCOVERY	13
2	THE 7 SECRETS IN THE GARDEN	25
3	THE MISSING LINK - PRAYER THERAPY FOR DEPRESSION	37
4	WHAT IS PRAYER THERAPY	57
5	PRAYER THERAPY vs. PSYCHOTHERAPY	67
6	PRELUDE TO PRAYER THERAPY (What Singer, Natalie Cole did)	75
7	DR. MINNIE CLAIBORNE'S C A R R Y TECHNIQUE (A new model)	83
8	A 21 DAY PRESCRIPTION OF PRAYER THERAPY	93

JOURNAL

INDEX

FOREWORD

I encourage you to read Dr. Claiborne's book because it is through my personal struggles that I have learned to respect the ongoing process that is required to overcome life's obstacles.

I am grateful to have acquired some of the tools that have helped me to face challenges more courageously. Healing is a choice. I believe that this book provides information and help that can transform your life.

It's amazing to see how beautifully and wonderfully life unfolds when we take proper care of ourselves spiritually, physically as well as emotionally. We can discover purpose and fulfill destiny.

Dr. Minnie Claiborne is a compassionate teacher, counselor and communicator. This book is from her heart to yours.

Dr. Claiborne, may God bless you and use you to bless others as you have blessed me.

With Love,

Natalie Cole

DEDICATION

I dedicate this book to every person who has ever been hurt emotionally. I know how you feel; more importantly, God knows how you feel and He will heal you. The principles and techniques that I share in this book were revealed to me by the Holy Spirit. I am a witness to this truth. "Jesus heals the brokenhearted" Luke 4:18.

Every time I experience a touch of God's glory, my first prayer is, "God let my children know the sweetness of your presence like this!" To my children, Shannon, Keturah and Emmanuel, remember, the people who hurt you cannot heal you. Forgive them and allow God to heal you and turn every bad experience into refined gold in your life that will reflect His Image. I love you!

I presently have three wonderful grand-sons: Justin, Keith Jr. and Kieron - (Ky-ran). Two wonderful son- in- loves: Keith Pender Sr. (Shannon) and Andre Kohl (Keturah). To the memory of my mother, Ferrol Busby; to my father, William Busby, and my 5 siblings who always make me feel like I'm so smart and beautiful! I love you. Walter (Toni) and kids: (Lashonda and (DelRoy) Hiram, India and (Nigel) Anthony (Ferrol Jr.) Mike, Sunshine (Darrell, Satinesha and Octavia) and Cynthia, (Wilfred Sr.) and kids: Destinee, Wilfred Jr. and Blue, excuse me, William.

To my faithful friends, assistants, helpers and prayer-partners: Evy E. E. (thank you for being so faithful). Eunice Rufunda, (thank you for agreeing with me that adversity will not cause us to lose our dignity. Vidella Waller, (thank you super woman). Alice Arthur (thank you for ALL of your help).

To my gracious, beautiful friend, Florence La Rue, (5th Dimension), continue to "let your light shine" you're a winner! Thanks for providing a home in the Valley for me. My spiritual daughter, Pastor Juanda Green, you are one of God's most precious jewels and all of my spiritual grand kids at New Visions, you all are…. (I'm speaking in tongues).

Dr. LaVerne Tolbert, you're so gifted, what a blessing you are to the Body of Christ, I love it when we praise together. Eric Stevens, (thank you for helping me with my naïve, blind-side).
Sister Menette Young, awesome servant of God, (I love you and I like you).

For anyone who God has used to help me to bring this message forward, thank you so much.
To any remaining members of Dr. Paul Trulin's family. God used him mightily to help birth out of me what God had placed within me while I attended Trinity School of the Bible.

To Pastor Jack Hayford and Matthew Barnett, thank you for mentoring me from afar. Pastor Hayford, thank God that you're on the planet! Thank you my sister- friend, Natalie Cole, you're a blessing to the world. God's not through with you yet-your best is yet to come! Thank you Allan Sealy for your wonderful gifts and talents (your accent) and for "working with me."

INTRODUCTION

Do you sometimes feel like the "real" you is somewhere buried beneath constricting, confining feelings of insecurity, fears, sadness, shame, anger, disappointment, discourage-ment, frustration, the pain of rejection, abandonment, betrayal or abuse?

Maybe you don't know exactly what's wrong with you but you don't feel like you're functioning to your full potential, something invisible, just beneath the surface of your consciousness is restricting you.

I lived with many of these feelings until about twenty years ago. I didn't know what was wrong with me, but I felt "not okay." To most people, I looked and behaved normally. I was successful; I had four degrees and was working on my doctorate; my handsome (deceased) husband earned a great income, we had two beautiful daughters, a big house and I had a brand new Mercedes. But I felt very insecure and battled with bouts of depression.

The best way I can describe my deepest emotional unhappiness was 'I felt apologetic for even being alive'. That may seem like a strange way to describe it, but it's the way I felt. Early one morning during my private prayer time I discovered why.

I got out of bed at four A.M. to have private prayer and worship. I said to God, "I don't know what's wrong with me, but I don't feel okay inside, will you help me?" In an instant I felt as if I was in a dream, watching a movie. I saw a young woman. She looked familiar, but I couldn't readily recognize who she was. As I continued looking at her, I could see that she was about nine months pregnant. Her head was bowed.

Suddenly I knew by revelation and realization that this young woman was my mother and the baby that she was carrying was me! Immediately thoughts and visions like the rewinding of a movie began in my mind. Somehow I knew what they all meant. My mother was pregnant with me, out of wedlock, in a small town. I also remembered something that she had begun to tell me once, but she only shared in bits and pieces. Concerning my father, she had said. "My cousins ran away and left me, he made me…." She left it at that. I also remembered once in her distress and frustration, my grandmother, who raised me said, "…your own father disowns you…"

Understanding began to flood my consciousness. My mother was 'acquaintance raped' in a very small town. The one thing that every young lady in that community knew was to not get pregnant and bring shame on her family. My mother felt hurt, ashamed, scorned and rejected. I was conceived and born with those same feelings of shame and rejection. This is sometimes referred to as a transference of spirits, some would even call it a 'generational curse'.

When a married couple has a child, family and friends 'celebrate' with them. They have baby showers, friends and family go to the hospital and the home with congratulations and welcoming gifts. My poor mother could only 'wish that I did not exist'. She could only bow her head in shame.

INTRODUCTION

That we human beings are a tripartite - spirit, soul and body, is a mystery to comprehend, but evidently we are. There are some things that we discover intellectually, (through our soul) some things we discover through our five senses, (our body) and there are other things that are intuitive or instinctive, that are revealed through our (spirit). I will discuss this in more detail later in the book.

During my time of prayer and worship some things were 'revealed' to me that I did not know intellectually neither through education or experience. God opened my understanding. From that experience, I began to learn the powerful process of how to minister emotional healing to myself and I have subsequently taught hundreds of other people how to be healed and free from pains of the past, present and future.

PRAYER THERAPY "STOP HURTING"
has a tri-fold application:

• Stop hurting - stop and find healing for the things that are hurting you.

• Stop hurting – stop hurting yourself (through unproductive, self-destructive behaviors) because you experienced hurt.

• Stop hurting- stop hurting others because someone hurt you.

If you've ever been hurt mentally and emotionally and

sincerely want God to help you, this book is for you! Let your hope be renewed and your faith be restored. No matter what happened to bring dis-ease to your soul (mind will, emotions), and no matter how long ago or how recently these things occurred, you can be healed and free... of ANYTHING! I'll teach you how in this book.

Love & Blessings

Dr. Minnie Claiborne

CHAPTER ONE
The Discovery

The following story illustrates how a "successful" young man discovered the need to stop hurting himself and the people whom he loved.

It was April in Alabama. The smells of blooming Dogwoods and wild Honeysuckles mixed with faint whiffs of Evergreens to form a fragrant, sensory bouquet as Kieron drove, windows down, around the coarsely paved, country road to Eliska. Gardner was dead and Kieron was going straight to the little country church to attend his funeral.

This was a different world from the fast-paced, stress-filled life that he lived as a businessman in Newport Beach, California. The Golden state had beckoned him after he completed a three year tour in the Navy, followed by a degree in Business Law. His education had paid off, he was rich! It was in Law school that he had met his Sue, his soon to be ex-wife. She had been a student at a nearby university, but one day she was on "his turf," doing research at the law library. When their eyes met, he instantly knew that he never wanted to be farther away from her than the next room. They were married a year and a half later.

Where had the years gone? What cold storm could have drenched the warm fire of their fervent love? Maybe it wasn't a big storm, just too many little showers; the missed dinners, his trips out of town, their not listening to each other. He spent too much time away from the family, building the business, things just got out of control. Their two young children, Breanna six, and Brian seven were suffering because of the tension. Sue said that he was 'emotionally disconnected' from her and the kids. What did that mean, emotionally disconnected?

Kieron was aware that his health was suffering also. Lately he had been feeling like a child, wanting to get off of life's carousel, but he didn't know how to make it stop. He was only thirty-five years old but his rapidly receding hairline and specks of grey hinted fifty.

Back here in Alabama, life seemed to have slowed down. How could the same twenty-four hours, seem like forty-eight in California and only twelve in Alabama?

Upon entering the door of the cool, white brick building, Kieron took a long, deep breath. It smelled like home. He recognized the voice of his cousin, Dutch; she was singing the opening song.

"A~mazing grace, how sweet the sound

A crisply dressed usher escorted Kieron to a reserved seat.

that saved a wretch, like me.

Kieron relaxed.

I once was lost but now I'm found
Was blind but now I see.

His mind drifted back on the rhythm of the song.

Through many dan-gers toils and snares
I have already come.
Twas grace that brought me safe thus far
And grace will lead me on.

He was thirteen years old when Gardner moved a few yards down the road. His father had died four months earlier.

His mother had explained how the lively sixty-nine year old was a third or fourth great-grand uncle or some genealogical combination that he could not remember. He immediately became fond of the wise old man with squinted eyes and an unsmiling but pleasant face. He looked like family, but different somehow. It was quite fascinating to see how Gardner could laugh while hardly moving his mouth. It was as if he wanted his laughter to water his own soul rather than to have it float away in the wind. Gardner was not very tall, maybe 5 feet 6 inches; that somehow made him seem more accessible.

Kieron tasted tears as he smiled, remembering the many times after school, when he walked down the graveled driveway and hopped onto Gardner's front porch. He would be greeted by the sound of tinkling ice cubes swimming in sync with bright yellow lemon slices in a large pitcher of iced tea. With calloused hands, Gardner would carefully fill two large glasses; one for Kieron and one for himself. After taking big swallows of the sweet, amber nectar, the two would always go out back to a little patch of land behind Gardner's house where year after year he grew the same seven plants.

Kieron sat on the second row from the front. Typical southern style, the casket was opened at the end of the ceremony. Even in death he could not accurately distinguish Gardner's ethnicity. He had coarse, thick grey hair that used to be jet black. Gardner said that was because he had Indian blood in him. He attributed his almond shaped eyes to his Asian ancestry, his quick wit, Irish. His strong masculine confidence came from his African blood, he laughed. Gardner said, "Son, out of one blood, the good Lord made all mankind." Gardner had lots of 'words of wisdom' like that.

"...and grace will lead us on."

Kieron decided to not go to the grave side committal service. He would rather remember Gardner's life. He was not ready to say good-bye yet.

His car seemed to automatically turn in the direction of Gardner's house. His feet instinctively carried him to the backyard, the place of memories that would last beyond death.

Eyes surveying the little plot of land that Gardner cared for so diligently and referred to as his *'life garden'*, Kieron stooped down. He picked up several fists full of dirt and let them slide slowly through his hand. He gazed intently at the trickles of sand and small rocks as if they held secrets that would connect him to Gardner. Why did Gardner grow only seven plants in his garden and why those particular seven things?

Kieron stood up. He looked at the withering Rose bushes, once full of vibrant, brilliant roses. They once made a floriferous semicircular fence around the peripheral of the garden. The Potato plants lay flattened by the spring rains and the Runner peanut plants were reduced to dead stubby stems. He looked at the spot where the Spinach was usually planted-only decaying remains. Even the usually lively Fig tree seemed to be in repose.

Opposite the Fig tree was Gardner's prized Anjou Pear tree. In its own private corner, supported by a crude trellis were the remains of his Muscadine Grape vines. This was the whole of the old man's horticultural occupation. Why did he call this his "life garden"?

Whenever Kieron had shared a problem with the old man, he would always counsel him in the garden; like the time he forgot his girlfriend's sixteenth birthday. She cried and refused to speak to him for a week. Kieron felt awful. The old man just put a friendly arm across the young man's shoulders and said "it'll be alright, come on let's check on the roses, I think I spotted a few aphids this morning."

That day Gardner seemed to be extra patient as he taught Kieron how to care for roses. He explained how they need lots of warm sunshine, and a generous supply of nurturing with nitrogen, potassium and phosphorus, along with careful watering. Do that, Gardner had said with a chuckle and they'll give you back lots of love in the form of beauty and an unforgettable aroma. Funny how he was remembering it all now, he thought that he was hardly listening that day so long ago. By sunset when Kieron left Gardner, the problem with his girlfriend was not solved, but he knew a lot about roses and he had to admit, he felt much better.

Come to think of it, Gardner always had a way of making him feel better; like during those difficult days when he was dealing with his father's death. That counseling session took place in the potato patch, ugh! They had dug up a few potatoes and thrown them into a sack. Kieron reached underneath one plant and put his hand into the mushy, smelly shell of a rotten potato. Just thinking about it almost brought back that horrible smell. As they washed their hands, Gardner explained that the potatoes on that plant had obviously been stricken with deadly blight. He had to remove the entire infected plant away from the healthy ones or it would ruin the entire crop.

The day he got the lesson on how to grow and take care of Peanuts was during the week of his eighteenth birthday; he was trying to decide what to do with his life.

Kieron took a long last look at this special place before he got back into his car to drive to his aunt's house to join the rest of the family. Upon entering the house, his mother handed him a copy of Gardner's will. The old man had left everything to Kieron. Through tear-hazed eyes, he looked at the signature on the crinkled scroll. Below his signature was scrawled P.S. "Don't try to re-grow my garden, bid it farewell and if you want the best chance for happiness in this life, you must be sure to take care of your own garden, it's your life." It was signed, Ted Gardner.

Gardner was actually his name? He thought that the old man was called Gardner because of his peculiar *"life garden"* with its seven different plants. Kieron looked out of the wide picture window of his aunt's house. What did Gardner mean, "Be sure to take care of your own garden"? He didn't have a garden.

Instinctively Kieron knew that Gardner wanted him to see something or KNOW something and the secret was in the old man's garden. He kissed his mom affectionately on the cheek, telling her he'd be right back.

Scroll in hand, Kieron ran the few blocks to Gardner's house and into the back yard. He looked anxiously around as if for a hidden treasure. He had the eerie feeling that someone was watching him. He did not know what he was looking for but he knew that he would recognize it when he found it.

The door key was in the same place; under a rusty, upside down coffee can near the back porch. Inside the house everything was neat and orderly just the way Gardner liked it. What he was looking for was not in the house it was in the garden. Twilight was descending. He was seized with anticipation as he headed for the old shed at the edge of the garden. He stepped inside and pulled on the light string. Dim light flooded the shed. Perhaps Gardner had left some kind of buried treasure somewhere in the garden; maybe he left clues in the shed. He looked around. There was nothing unusual, just a lot of rusty old cans and sacks; things that only held meaning for Gardner...wait there was something scrawled on the wall in the same hand writing that was on the scroll that he still held in his hand. It was Gardner's. Kieron pushed aside a couple of bins that Gardner used to collect mulch. He wiped the dust off of the wall. There in the old man's handwriting were the names of the seven plants that he grew in his garden.

They were listed vertically, and beside each was another word or phrase in parenthesis. His list looked like this:

Spinach   (spirit, soul, body)

Pears   (proper care of self)

Peanuts   (purpose on earth)

Grapes   (good health, mind and body)

Figs   (financial prosperity)

Roses   (relationships with people)

Potatoes   (pains of the past)

Revelation hit his mind like a tsunami. It seemed to wash away a veil from Kieron's eyes. He could not believe that it

took him twenty-two years to understand what Gardner began teaching him when he was just thirteen years old. He had not been teaching the boy about gardening at all, but about LIFE! No wonder he explained the delicacy of Roses when he had trouble with his girl friend.
The wise old man even knew that the bitterness and anger that Kieron felt because of his father's death were like those rotting potatoes, infecting his soul. That's also why they always tossed the baseball or did push-ups facing the grape vines-Grapes….good health. Kieron raised his eyes toward the ceiling, "Thank you Gardner," he whispered. As he looked up, he noticed a red tin box, the size of a shoe box on the shelf above the writing. Among other things, he noticed seven little booklets, each held together with twine. He thumbed through them and recognized the now familiar handwriting that was Gardner's. He untied one of them and read the first few lines…..Relationships are like Roses, they die in the cold …another read…Rotting Potatoes are like Past Pains, the blight infects every thing it touches.

Kieron stood in awed silence for a while. Now he understood. Gardner had left him a treasure that was priceless- wisdom! He did have a garden, his life; and he had left his Roses, (His relationship with Sue and the children), out in the cold. He had never talked to anyone about it, but he also had rotting potatoes, (unresolved anger at his father, not just for dying, but for mistreating his mother while he was alive). He tucked the box under his arms, turned off the light, closed the door and began to walk slowly back toward his Aunt Roxie's house. By now, twilight was giving way to darkness, but he could see clearly. His partners, Keith and Justin, could handle the business for a while; he had a different kind of work to do.

As he walked, the heels of his shoes seemed to be drumming an old song that Gardner sang or hummed constantly.

> "Now let us have a little talk with Jesus, let us
> tell Him all about our trouble.
> He will hear our faintest, cry
> and He'll answer by and by.
> Just a little talk with Jesus makes it right, all right!"

Summary of Chapter One

Thirty-five year old Kieron built what had the appearance of a successful life for himself, but he was not happy. His family was falling apart, his health was failing, he was frustrated and miserable most of the time.
While at his home town in Eliska, Alabama, attending his childhood mentor's funeral, he discovered that the old man, Gardner, had used his real life garden to try and teach the younger man about real life problems.

Kieron discovered that the 7 plants in Gardner's garden represented the 7 foundational areas of human life. Each needed to be properly understood and maintained. He realized that he had given a lot of attention to his Figs (finances); but had sorely neglected his Roses (relationships) as well as his Grapes (good health). He began his journey back home with clearer vision and new determination.

The purpose of this chapter is to illustrate the fact that

success in one area of our lives, while neglecting another produces imbalance, and prohibits true happiness and fulfillment. A person may have good mental and physical health, for example, but that same person may be extremely frustrated because they have no real sense of their life purpose and destiny. Kieron's financial success did not compensate for the neglect of his health and his relationship with his wife and children.

CHAPTER TWO
The Seven Secrets in the Garden

Kieron and Gardner's story illustrates a truth that was revealed to me which I will share with you. This knowledge will help you to forever manage the garden of your own life should you choose to apply it. During the past twenty-five years of personal growth and through counseling and ministering to hundreds of other people, I discovered that all of life's problems fall into SEVEN general symbiotic categories. We may have a hundred scenarios, or situations, but if we can categorize them into their seven basic core components and learn to manage them, we will have a happier, healthier, more fulfilled, successful and dynamic, life on earth. The 7 areas must be consistently maintained, nurtured and repaired as needed.

I have tested this many times over the years, with hundreds of people and its truth is continually confirmed. There are SEVEN basic, symbiotic categories into which ALL human problems fall. Our lives can be compared to a garden, the 7 areas, like 7 plants. It is our individual responsibility to repair, nurture and maintain them. In the 7 little booklets, Gardner revealed these 7 secrets to Kieron.

SECRET NUMBER ONE - We must understand that
WE ARE SPIRIT, SOUL AND BODY.

SECRET NUMBER TWO - We must have
A PROPER RELATIONSHIP WITH OUR SELF.

SECRET NUMBER THREE - We must know
OUR PURPOSE AND DESTINY.

SECRET NUMBER FOUR - We must maintain
GOOD MENTAL AND PHYSICAL HEALTH.

SECRET NUMBER FIVE - We must have
SUFFICIENT FINANCIAL PROSPERITY.

SECRET NUMBER SIX - We must have harmonious
RELATIONSHIPS WITH SIGNIFICANT OTHERS.

SECRET NUMBER SEVEN - We must be HEALED OF
PAINS FROM THE PAST.

These Seven symbiotic areas affect all human beings; it is within these seven areas that hurts, abuses, disappointments and the like occur. Like a prized garden, our lives are in consistent need of Maintenance, Nurturing or Repair in one or several of these areas. Our neglect of these is wreaking havoc in the human race. We see its devastation in an avalanche of broken homes, domestic violence, depression, fear, confusion, pornography, drug and alcohol addiction, violence, anger, molestations, low self esteem, sexual, verbal, mental and emotional abuse rejection, abandonment, the list goes on. Neither ritual nor religion have been able to impede it.

SECRET NUMBER ONE - WE ARE COMPRISED OF SPIRIT SOUL AND BODY

Let's look at the first category and see what kind of problems fall into that category. As human beings we are spirit, soul and body. Hundreds of us neglect one or the other of these areas all of the time. There are those of us who are very physically fit, but our spirit and soul may be suffering, which will cause suffering in all of the other areas of our lives. Remember these seven areas are symbiotic-different, but interdependent. This is also true of our tri-partite-3 part nature. Our spirit, soul and body are distinct in identity, but dependent in function. If you neglect one the other suffers.

Look at it logically. All of us know that going to the gym or working out vigorously everyday does not increase one's intellect. In fact that is not the purpose of physical activity. Likewise reading books, and studying without exercise will not make you physically fit. These are activities that enhance your intellect, not your body.

Also neither physical fitness nor intellectual stimulation alone will feed your spirit, it needs spiritual food. Among these are: Prayer, Meditation in the Holy Scriptures, and consistent Worship. This is our individual responsibility.

THE SOUL

As a person we are comprised of spirit, soul and body. Research distinguishes three parts of the soul also, they are:

mind, will and emotions. Our minds take in and process cognitive data. Our wills make decisions based on this data or information and our emotions are the feelings we have in response to both of these. For example. I see a snake, my mind says "danger," my will says, "move away from danger," my emotions feel fear. All of these are actions of the SOUL. These processes happen so fast that they seem like one action and reaction, but our brains are so wonderfully and fearfully made and our responses so well-synchronized that we do not take note of the minute details of the process.

The soul has perhaps been the most neglected area of twenty-first century people. People have had MANY experiences that caused them great emotional pain, and the pain still remains.

We put band aids on our scraped knees, we have surgery and take pills for our physical infirmities, but other than detrimental behaviors, the majority of our society does little more than take a pill to escape their deep emotional pain and traumas; never truly accessing the origin or the root of the emotional trauma and administering healing at the place of pain. You can learn to find healing at the points of pain through PRAYER THERAPY. Traditional therapy can sometimes locate the point of pain. PRAYER THERAPY invites the 'God who heals' into the process. You can do it alone or with someone who you trust. It does not have to be a professional.

*However, if you or someone you are helping are too ill, or are in crisis or an experience is too painful to handle alone, or is life-threatening, do not hesitate to go to a reputable hospital, Psychologist or Psychiatrist. You can still employ PRAYER THERAPY in the hospital if that's what you have to do.

SECRET NUMBER TWO - WE NEED PROPER RELATIONSHIP WITH SELF

I am taking time to review these seven areas of human problems and experiences because it will help you to identify your problems. You can then begin the process of repairing, nurturing or maintaining them properly. You will no longer try to fix a spiritual problem with a physical remedy, or an emotional problem with a physical remedy, etc.

Having a proper relationship with yourself will either positively or negatively affect every other area of your life. Poor self-esteem and poor self-image have caused people to die from anorexia and bulimia, to disfigure themselves through numerous plastic surgeries and more. Poor self worth has caused sexual promiscuity, repeated abusive relationships, lack of job success and various forms of victimization. Anger and unforgiveness are causes of heart disease and other life-threatening maladies.

No amount of money, physical attractiveness, or even good relationships with significant others will fix the problem. You and I need to know why we don't feel okay. That's what I needed and I found the answer. If you were molested, raped, abused, rejected or abandoned, and it warped your self image, self worth, or self-esteem; proper application of my prayer therapy techniques can help you.

SECRET NUMBER THREE - WE NEED TO HAVE A SENSE OF OUR PURPOSE & DESTINY

People who don't understand their purpose, the thing that they do that is so fulfilling to them, so suited for them, that doing it is like constantly re-newing oneself. Researchers say that most people have heart failure on Monday mornings. Some believe that its because so many actually hate their jobs. We are programmed to learn a profession that will bring us good money, even if we hate what we do.

It is well worth it to take some time out, think about what you have a real passion for and find a way to do it either as a vocation or an avocation. Some professionals, even lawyers have changed their professions in order to find a more fulfilling career.

Think about it? What do you really like to do? What is your real passion? Do you feel deep down that this a divine gift, placed within you by God? Is there any way to pursue it?

Back to SECRET NUMBER ONE. The only one who can reveal your purpose and destiny is the one who designed you. Deliberate, intimate time in prayer, scripture reading and just spending time with God is the secret to knowing your purpose and destiny. Consider Jeremiah 1:5-10 and especially Genesis Chapter 32. Jacob "wrestled" with an angel of the Lord all night...until his name was changed and his destiny revealed.

SECRET NUMBER FOUR - WE NEED GOOD MENTAL AND PHYSICAL HEALTH

One Christian lady quoted a scripture, concerning her weight as she sat on the couch eating potato chips. "I will lose weight because the Bible says that I can do all things through Christ who gives me strength." The answer came back. "Let's begin by me giving you strength to throw away that bag of chips." Quoting scriptures without applying action will not produce results. "Faith without works is dead." Some people over spiritualize and neglect their personal responsibility to employ healthy eating, exercises and other common sense, health practices such as drinking enough water and getting enough sleep.

We seem to be living in an age of 'magical thinking'. We want instantaneous results when we pray. Prayer does not take away our personal responsibility to do our part.

Mental health researchers attribute as much as 85% of mental illness to unforgiveness. Forgiveness is a choice of the will, which you will remember is a part of the soul. Soul= mind+will+emotions. Prayer therapy will teach you how to forgive without relieving responsibility from the guilty party... It will also teach you how to separate healing for emotional woundedness from forgiveness.

We have to do certain things to protect our minds, so that the injustices, traumas and stresses do not cause mental illness which will incapacitate and further victimize us. Learning to process the pain through prayer therapy will help to protect your mental health. Our society is rich with information on how to maintain good physical health.

SECRET NUMBER FIVE - WE NEED SUFFICIENT FINANCIAL PROSPERITY

You may be surprised to discover that a healthy spiritual life can lead to honest, legitimate financial prosperity. The Bible says in Duet. 8:18 "But thou shall remember the Lord thy God, for it is He that giveth thee power to get wealth..." The Bible is filled with insight and wisdom on how to obtain prosperity and good success. Lack of financial prosperity causes stress and mental problems, as well as problems in society. But again, if we're not careful, we can blame other things and not get to the root cause of our money issues.

What sense does it make to "get drunk or high" as a way of escaping your financial responsibility? Some people even spend more money. They do "shopping therapy," which only makes matters worse. Perhaps through feeding your spirit (prayer, reading and meditating on the truths in the scriptures, attendance at a Christ-centered Church or Fellowship), you will get a God-inspired idea for a business or an idea on how to go back to school or get a trade. Read Joshua 1: 8. Remember, all seven areas of our 'life garden' are interrelated.

Obedience to God's directions was the key to Abraham, Isaac and Jacob's wealth. NOTE: He told them how and where to DO BUSINESS. As covenant people, they obeyed and prospered. Read Genesis: Chapters 15, 26, 30, 31 and Galatians 3:6-18. Abraham was already rich when he began tithing. His motive for giving to the high priest was not to become wealthy. Selah.

Not only will attending to our spiritual health help us financially, when we are mentally and physically alert, we are more able to take advantage of any opportunity that might come along. Some people have sabotaged their own success because of poor self worth or because they have problems with our next of the seven areas-relationships with other people.

Can you see how we need to diligently take inventory of all seven areas of our lives consistently? A regular program of prayer therapy will do this for you. You can make the decision to do it yourself without spending thousands of dollars and years of time in therapy with someone else.

SECRET NUMBER SIX - WE NEED GOOD RELATIONSHIPS WITH OTHERS

This one is especially challenging because most of the hurts that we experience come through significant others. It is also within the context of interpersonal relationships that we are forced to confront our own flaws. It is in this area where the soul's battles rage. The will to forgive argues with the pain of our emotions. The memories of our minds fuel the feeling of our emotions, so that only the strength of our spirits are able to so influence our minds that our wills choose forgiveness over vengeance, love over hatred, and ultimately sanity over insanity.

The difficult decision to forgive is made in the court rooms of our souls, but the crimes against us were most often perpetrated in the vulnerable arena of relationships with people we love. In PRAYER THERAPY we forgive and release people who harmed us, but we know that God will punish them, and they will reap what they have sown. Sometimes its hard for us to forgive because we feel that the person is getting away with it. Holding them hostage in your own mind only hurts you. PRAYER THERAPY offers a better way.

SECRET NUMBER SEVEN - WE NEED TO BE HEALED OF HURTS AND PAINS FROM THE PAST

Pains of the past are not in the past. Unless they're healed, they come with us into the present and will go with us into our futures.

Gardner compared pains from the past to rotting potatoes. Potatoes that have brownish or grayish patches and appear slightly sunken indicate infection with 'blight'. Such potatoes will either become dry and mummified or rot completely. If left untreated the disease will spread rapidly to other plants and in a short while, all of the plants will rot and collapse.

An infected potato may look healthy enough to be stored with other potatoes until the unpleasant odor signals a problem, and is detected. The bacteria will cause decomposition in the affected potato and will aggressively destroy all of the other potatoes that it touches.

Similarly many people appear to be normal, but repressed hurts, abuses, and the like will eventually ooze out, contaminate one's thoughts and feelings and cause destructive behaviors. Without intervention, people who have repressed pain will decompose in various ways and will likely contaminate other people with whom they come in contact.

This is clearly demonstrated in the horrible, raging epidemic of domestic violence. According to FBI statistics, more women are hurt and killed by an abusive partner or ex-partner than by drownings, car accidents, rape and murder by strangers and victims in the Vietnam War combined. Read that again! This happens because the abuser has not taken responsibility to go through the necessary process to get his soul healed. Consequently many young children see their mothers cursed, kicked, slapped, thrown down stairs, stabbed, shot and killed. It happens every 9 seconds. Physical, emotional and sexual abuse of both boys and girls is also common where spousal abuse is present.

'Blight of the soul' is caused by the unresolved, unhealed pain of traumatic emotional experiences. This malady robs the infected individual of love, peace and happiness and causes him or her to infect and afflict pain on those with whom they have close contact. I've heard stories that you would not believe!

I've looked into hundreds of tear-drenched adult faces who have lived for years with the pain of childhood verbal, mental, emotional and sexual abuse; men and women who were raped and molested by their own fathers. Women, who have been brutally beaten, kicked, stalked, tied up and held hostage and more by their 'husbands'! The human soul was not designed to carry such a heavy burden.

Summary of Chapter Two

Chapter Two expands the revelation of the 7 symbiotic categories of human experiences in detail. People are more prone to take care of the areas of life that are more obvious, such as physical health problems or financial matters, but matters of the spirit and soul are not readily visible, so those are often neglected except in extreme cases. The purpose of this chapter is to distinguish the 7 areas and to help us to realize that it is necessary to take proper care of all of them, especially the PAINS OF THE PAST. These are areas of the SOUL (mind, will, emotions) that have been hurt, abused, abandoned, rejected and traumatized and which need to be healed if we are to lead healthy, happy, productive lives and fulfill our God-ordained purpose on earth. Proper care of all seven of these areas of life will result in harmony or unity of Spirit, Soul and Body. I Thessalonians 5:23.

DEFINITION OF EMOTIONS- Any feeling, especially a strong or intense feeling, as of love, joy, fear, anger, hurt, hatred etc. often accompanied by complex physiological changes.

When Kieran's wife said that he was 'emotionally disconnected' from her and the children; she meant that he was not able to express strong feelings of love and care in a way that made them feel a part of him.

CHAPTER THREE
The Missing Link

In my introduction, I mentioned that during the time that I was "not feeling okay". I was not physically sick, we had money and "things," my martial and family relationships were fine and I thank God that I had a wonderful relationship with Him. What was missing? What was missing was a proper relationship with MYSELF and MY PAST. This is the 'missing link' for many, many, many people.

According to the Center for Disease Control (CDC) over 65% of the American population suffers from depression. Forty -five per cent of the population is taking some type of psychotropic drug, which can be very dangerous. Bi-polar, schizophrenia and various psychosis and neuroses have become acceptable in our society. The mental health system is overwhelmed. A young lady called a mental health center recently explaining that she felt suicidal and on the verge of returning to a 17 year crack cocaine habit. They told her that they could see her in two weeks!

Many people try to use their religion to 'cover up' rather than to 'pray through' the healing process. They feel guilty for having emotional problems because they think that their faith is weak. They fail to properly appropriate scriptures such as is found in Luke 4:18 Jesus said, "The spirit of the Lord is upon me, because He has anointed me to preach the gospel to the poor; He has sent Me to heal the brokenhearted, to proclaim liberty to the captives and recovery of sight to the blind, to set at liberty those who are oppressed; to proclaim the acceptable year of the Lord."

Others use the scripture in II Corinthians 5:17 as a justification for not seeking God's healing for their emotional pain and traumas of the past. The verse reads: "Therefore if anyone is in Christ, he is a new creation; old things have passed away; behold all things have become new." Thank God for this revelation. When we are born again we pass from death to life. We are now reconciled to God, made alive in our spirits. We now have the capacity and access to God to be transformed in our minds and one day to put on our incorruptible new bodies.

Just like you and I did not get an instantaneous new body that we can see, at the time of our new birth; we likewise did not get our memories wiped out. If you were born again at age 20 and weighed 150 pounds, your spirit became new instantly, but your physical body did not change. Sometimes people have experienced instaneous healings at the time of the new birth; but all of us know of born-again people who are ill-yet they are a 'new creation'. However, they now have the privilege of praying for healing. If a person was molested at age 8, and born again at age 20, that memory is rarely wiped away. If God's healing is not invited into that specific place of pain, the mal-adjustive behavior as a result of the trauma will probably remain.

This is why there is so much confusion in the church world today. Many gifted and anointed people are bound, oppressed, addicted, abusers and criminal. In most cases, they have failed to adequately appropriate God's healing to their past abuses, pains, abandonment's, rejections, anger and traumas.

The Bible says in Psalm 34:19 "Many are the afflictions of the righteous, but the Lord delivers him out of them all": IF WE DENY THAT WE HAVE AFFLICTIONS, WE DENY GOD ACCESS TO DELIVER US OUT OF THEM.

I am not suggesting that we walk around agreeing with the enemy or our symptoms, or making a "bad confession." I am encouraging us to come with truth in our inward parts; bringing our troubled and broken hearts, and crying out to the almighty God, who is our healer, the one who restores our soul (mind, will, emotions). Psalms 23.

What do you want me to do for you?
This was the question that Jesus asked the man in the scriptures who was known as Blind Bartimaeus. This is an excellent story for those who take the position of "Well, God knows what I need, so I don't have to ask." In this illustration, found in Mark 10: 46-52. Blind Bartimaeus apparently a well-known blind man, who sat by the road side, begging, heard that Jesus was in the crowd. He began to cry out, "Jesus, Son of David, have mercy on me!" The more the crowd bade him be quiet, the more he cried out, "Son of David, have mercy on me!" (May we too cry out with such humility, faith, and resolve). His passion and sincerity attracted Jesus' attention. Jesus commanded the

blind man to come to him. The crowd then began to encourage him saying "be of good cheer, rise, he's calling you." Because Blind Bartimaeus ignored the criticism of the crowd and cried out to Jesus, Jesus in turn called out to him. It was obvious that the man was blind, and of course Jesus is Omniscient, but yet he asks blind Bartimaeus "What do you want me to do for you?" The blind man did not quote scriptures to Jesus, he said to Him, (with HUMILITY and RESPECT), "Raboni, that I may receive my sight." Jesus said to him, "Go your way; your faith has made you well."

Let us not deceive ourselves into thinking that we can ignore emotional pains and trauma and they will just go away. They will not. Sometimes just 'confessing healing scriptures' is not enough. We must come to the Lord, Jesus Christ, our Healer with humility, honor and respect. We must be humble enough to say, Lord it hurts right here! I understand prayer to mean COMMUNICATION with God, not just talking to God. Communication means you send and receive a message. In intimate relationship with God, we don't just arrogantly wave His word in His face and demand that He performs it. Jesus prayed in John chapter seventeen, that we would KNOW God. One of my favorite scriptures is Psalm 25:14 "The secret of the Lord is with those who fear Him; And He will show them His covenant." The word secret here means, counsel, counseling session, the word fear is worship, respect and honor, covenant is a promise or agreement.

It is in reverent, intimacy with God that we receive counseling and His answers concerning matters that we pray about. How many of your close friends do you communicate with by arrogantly "reminding them of what they said they would do"? It was in my intimate time of worship and fellowship with my Heavenly Father that I received the "keys" (secret) to my permanent emotional healing, keys that I am now sharing with you and thousands of others.

Far too many very gifted and 'anointed' people are bound and oppressed by various destructive habits and lifestyles as a result of unhealed wounds of the soul. Countless people, of all faiths are dying prematurely due to the drug abuse, heart disease, high blood pressure, alcoholism, depression and other deadly results of unhealed hurts. Others are going around in circles of pain year after year….like Hannah.

An Old Testament account of a woman named Hannah bears looking at. Hannah had a husband who loved her, she went to church, offered sacrifices, and seemed to not have any financial lack, but there was something else that she desired and it became an area of provocation by her adversary which caused Hannah to become depressed and bitter.

Like Hannah, you may be feeling challenged or frustrated right now because of things that have happened that are not as you desired or planned; or some things that you hoped, prayed and wished for may not have happened yet.

I promise you that God loves you and He will faithfully perform EVERYTHING that He has promised for your personal life if you will allow Him to.

Sometimes we have to wait until the "fullness of time" or "due season" for a promise to be fulfilled. Sometimes God is working out something bigger and better than we imagined. Remember He is working on your present life purpose on earth as well as things that impact your eternal life.
Let me give you an example by reviewing Hannah's story. Hannah was one of two women who were married to the same man (legally permitted then).

Hannah's husband loved her more, and gave her a double portion of everything, but Hannah's heart's desire was to have a child. Specifically, she longed to have a son. To make matters worse, the other wife, Peninnah kept getting pregnant and having children. Peninnah "provoked" and taunted Hannah sorely.

The other wife provoked and teased her to the point that she actually made Hannah sick! She grieved so much that She would only weep and not even be able to eat. She was miserable and depressed. The Bible says that she was in bitterness of soul.

Hannah was in this condition because she did not have what she wanted. She did not have a son.

The Bible also tells us that after going to The house of the Lord "year after year" Hannah still did not have what she desired.

You may be having a similar experience. Is there something that you have believed God for, year after year and it has not happened? Be encouraged! God will NEVER forget you. He may be trying to raise your perspective. Remember, He is concerned about your earthly life as well as your eternal life.

Let's look at what happened to Hannah. Remember, she had been sick and depressed for years because she wanted a son, and her adversary constantly taunted and provoked her. She had no peace. Having a son was her strong desire for many reasons.

The Bible goes on to say that one day as Hannah was praying, her perspective changed. It seems that as she cried out to God, her spirit glimpsed eternity. Immediately, her prayer changed. She no longer wanted a son just to please her husband, or to gain social status, or to prove her womanhood; not even to rub it in that mean old Peninnah's face. She abandoned the notion that God should answer her prayer because of her husband's service to God. Here is what she prayed: *Oh Lord of hosts, if thou wilt indeed look on the affliction of Thine handmaid and remember me, and not forget Thine handmaid, but wilt give unto Thine hand maid a man child, then I will give him unto the Lord all the days of his life…*

This time God answered Hannah's prayer. Why? I believe that her perspective changed. *Please read James 4: 1-10 concerning why our prayers are not answered (Ouch!).

I personally believe that our prayers are more effective when we find out what God wants to do and pray in agreement with His revealed will. Here is what I mean. We know in general what God's will is. It is written in His word (logos). But in specific situations, we may not immediately know the mind of God. In those instances, we need a (rhema) present and specific word from the Lord.

The apostle Paul tells us in the book of Romans, chapter 8, verses 26-28 that the Spirit helps our infirmities in prayer, for we know not how to pray as we ought…

I'll give you a personal example. A lady asked me to pray for her. She was in great anguish and misery. She was tormented because she could not sense the presence of God. She felt like she was in a fog, and had committed some terrible sin that she was unaware of. She had other symptoms also. She was depressed and nearly suicidal. She was desperate. I was visiting her state, and only had a few minutes to help her. There was no time for weekly counseling sessions.

I knew in general, of course that it was God's will to heal and comfort her, but this was not a case in which I could say a prayer and leave. I did not know how to pray (specifically), so I began to worship and praise the Lord for a few minutes. Almost immediately, the other gifts of the Holy Spirit (word of knowledge and word of wisdom) began to operate.

I asked her, "Linda, are you pregnant?" She gasped, "Yes! I just got the news a couple of weeks ago, how did you know?" I asked her, "Did your doctor prescribe iron supplements for you?" She gasped again in amazement. "How did you know that?" She asked. I asked again, "Have you been taking them?" She gasped, "No! But how do you know this?" I told her that the Holy Spirit had let me know that her problem was physical, her iron levels were low, and her hormones were adjusting.

She was gloriously relieved, and agreed that what I shared made perfect sense, and she had peace and would take her supplements and take care of her self properly physically.
You may wonder what that story has to do with you or with

Hannah. Well, I'll tell you. Sometimes we become 'stuck' on our expectation of how or when God should answer our prayers. Effective prayer occurs when we discern God's (specific and present will) in a situation, and agree with Him. His will is always good, whether we understand it or not. Remember Hannah's perspective changed and she received her son, after she offered him back to God, for His glory as well as her fulfillment. Its NOT just about us!

Remember that God is working on both earthly and eternal things. Look at what was happening in the Heavenly realm while Hannah was praying here on earth.

The Bible says that during that time, the Word of God was "rare." The sons of Eli the priest were horribly profaning the house of God. God needed a voice, God needed a prophet!

Look at how heaven and earth met; Hannah wanted a son, God needed a Prophet! Hannah's son, Samuel, became one of God's most honorable prophets and changed the nation of Israel. "Everything he prophesied, God brought it to pass." Read the entire account in I Samuel Chapters 1, 2, 3 and beyond. That's the kind of thing that can happen when we submit our wills to God's will in prayer.

What does all of this have to do with emotional wholeness?

Well many of us are "bitter of soul" because of things that have happened or that have not happened to us as we expected. God has promised that as we pray according to the will of God, "All things will work together for our good if we love God and are called according to His purpose."

Our SOUL is our MIND, WILL and EMOTIONS. Once we are born-again, our spirits are re-born; our souls must be transformed by the renewing of our minds and the healing of our emotions if we are willing to allow God to do it.

The lack of the above revelation has caused much confusion and heartbreak in many, many believers.

You and I and every person on earth have experienced some kind of emotional pain. Jesus is called "Wonderful, Counselor, mighty God Prince of Peace, Healer." He is ready and willing to be all of that to us if we cry out to him and admit our afflictions. We can then move on to fulfill purpose and destiny in a greater way than we anticipated.

God is by passing some of us because of our ATTITUDES. We are not humble. We are whining and complaining, comparing and envying, or the adversary is provoking us sore, or the emotional pain keeps getting swallowed down while we go to church year after year.

During my prayer time, I saw a vision of two women at prayer. One was a very poor woman. She was on her knees, dressed in rags, she with tears, was presenting her petitions to God.

The other woman was meticulously attired, every hair in place. She sat, head high, legs crossed in the presence of a Holy God. She swept her hand across the desk and plopped her resume down, demanding that God perform for her, based on "Who she was."

God performs based on WHO HE IS and His love, grace, and mercy in relationship to us, not because of our goodness or righteousness. Yes, all that He has is ours and He has said He will freely give it to us, but He is a sovereign God and is to be respected, honored and worshipped.

Everything in your house belongs to your children basically, but how would you respond to the one who would stick his chest in your face and demand what he wants, rather than asking reverently and respectfully?

Emotional wholeness is ours. Let us ask for it humbly, reverently and respectfully.

God wants to stop the pain. If it's the pain of rejection, abandonment, abortion, molestation, rape, divorce, death, never been married, abuse, domestic violence, discrimination, mental illness, physical infirmity, broken relationships, wayward children, anything that hurts us.

DEPRESSION: AN AVOIDABLE EPIDEMIC?

The best use of PRAYER THERAPY is as a PREVENTATIVE tool. If we learn to CARRY our hurts, pains, disappointments and grief to our Lord who came to earth to heal our broken hearts; many mental diseases and disorders can be avoided.

Feeling sad or down occasionally is pretty much a normal part of life. But when emptiness and despair overwhelm you and won't go away, it may be depression. More than just the temporary "blues," the lows of depression make it tough to function and enjoy life like... Hobbies and friends don't interest you like they used to; you're exhausted all the time; and just getting through the day can be overwhelming. When you're depressed, things may feel hopeless, but with help and support you can get better.

We all go through ups and downs in our mood. Sadness is a normal reaction to life's struggles, setbacks, and disappointments. Some people describe depression as "living in a black hole" or having a feeling of impending doom. However, some depressed people don't feel sad at all-instead, they feel lifeless, empty, and apathetic.

Whatever the symptoms, depression is different from normal sadness in that it engulfs your day-to-day life, interfering with your ability to work, study, eat, sleep, and have fun. The feelings of helplessness, hopelessness, and worthlessness are intense and unrelenting, with little, if any, relief.

Common signs and symptoms of depression

- **Feelings of helplessness and hopelessness.** A bleak outlook-nothing will ever get better and there's nothing you can do to improve your situation.
- **Loss of interest in daily activities.** No interest in former hobbies, pastimes, social activities, or sex. You've lost your ability to feel joy and pleasure.
- **Appetite or weight changes.** Significant weight loss or weight gain-a change of more than 5% of body weight in a month.
- **Sleep changes.** Either insomnia, especially waking in the early hours of the morning, or oversleeping (also known as hypersomnia).

- **Irritability or restlessness.** Feeling agitated, restless, or on edge. Your tolerance level is low; everything and everyone gets on your nerves.
- **Loss of energy.** Feeling fatigued, sluggish, and physically drained. Your whole body may feel heavy, and even small tasks are exhausting or take longer to complete.
- **Self-loathing.** Strong feelings of worthlessness or guilt. You harshly criticize yourself for perceived faults and mistakes.
- **Concentration problems.** Trouble focusing, making decisions, or remembering things.
- **Unexplained aches and pains.** An increase in physical complaints such as headaches, back pain, aching muscles, and stomach pain.

IF YOU ARE FEELING SUICIDAL...

When you're feeling extremely depressed or suicidal, problems don't seem temporary - they seem overwhelming and permanent. But with time, you will feel better, especially if you reach out for help. If you are feeling suicidal, know that there are many people who want to support you during this difficult time, so please reach out for help!

Read **Coping with Suicidal Thoughts and Getting Help** or call **1-800-273-TALK** now or visit www.Helpguide.org

Depression and Suicide

Depression is a major risk factor for suicide. The deep despair and hopelessness that goes along with depression can make suicide feel like the only way to escape the pain. Thoughts of death or suicide are a serious symptom of depression, so take any suicidal talk or behavior seriously. It's not just a warning sign that the person is thinking about suicide: it's a cry for help.

Warning signs of suicide include:

- Talking about killing or harming one's self.
- Expressing strong feelings of hopelessness or being trapped.
- An unusual preoccupation with death or dying.
- Acting recklessly, as if they have a death wish (e.g. speeding through red lights).
- Calling or visiting people to say goodbye.
- Getting affairs in order (giving away prized possessions, tying up loose ends).
- Saying things like "Everyone would be better off without me" or "I want out."
- Sudden switch from being extremely depressed to acting calm and happy.

Depression often looks different in men and women, than in young people and older adults. An awareness of these differences helps ensure that the problem is recognized and treated.

Suicide has become the third leading cause of death among

teens and young adults in the United States. Left untreated, teen depression can lead to problems at home and school, drug abuse, self-loathing-even irreversible tragedy such as homicidal violence or suicide.

Depression in teens can look very different from depression in adults. The following symptoms of depression are more common in teenagers than in their adult counterparts:

- **Irritable or angry mood** - As noted above, irritability, rather than sadness, is often the predominant mood in depressed teens.
A depressed teenager may be grumpy, hostile, easily frustrated, or prone to angry outbursts.
- **Unexplained aches and pains** - Depressed teens frequently complain about physical ailments such as headaches or stomachaches. If a thorough physical exam does not reveal a medical cause, these aches and pains may indicate depression.
- **Extreme sensitivity to criticism** - Depressed teens are plagued by feelings of worthlessness, making them extremely vulnerable to criticism, rejection, and failure. This is a particular problem for "over-achievers."
- **Withdrawing from some, but not all people** - While adults tend to isolate themselves when depressed, teenagers usually keep up at least some friendships. However, teens with depression may socialize less than before, pull away from their parents, or start hanging out with a different crowd.

Effects of teen and young adult depression

The negative effects of teenage depression go far beyond a melancholy mood. Many rebellious and unhealthy behaviors or attitudes in teenagers are actually indications of depression. See the table below for some of the ways in which teens "act out" or "act in" in an attempt to cope with their emotional pain:

Untreated Depression Can Lead to...

Problems at school	Depression can cause low energy and concentration difficulties. At school, this may lead to poor attendance, a drop in grades or frustration with schoolwork in a formerly good student.
Running away	Many depressed teens run away from home or talk about running away. Such attempts are usually a cry for help.
Substance abuse	Teens may use alcohol or drugs in an attempt to "self-medicate" their depression. Unfortunately, substance abuse only makes things worse.
Low self-esteem	Depression can trigger and intensify feelings of ugliness, shame, failure and unworthiness.
Eating disorders	Anorexia, bulimia, binge eating and yo-yo dieting are often signs of unrecognized depression.
Internet addiction	Teens may go online to escape from their problems. But excessive computer use only increases their isolation and makes them more depressed.
Self-injury	Cutting, burning, and other kinds of self-mutilation are almost always associated with depression. To learn more, see Helpguide's Self-Injury.
Reckless behavior	Depressed teens may engage in dangerous or high-risk behaviors, such as reckless driving, out-of-control drinking and unsafe sex.
Violence	Some depressed teens (usually boys who are the victims of bullying) become violent. As in the case of the Columbine High School massacre, self-hatred and a wish to die can erupt into violence and homicidal rage.
Suicide	Teens who are seriously depressed often think, speak, or make "attention-getting" attempts at suicide. Suicidal thoughts or behaviors should always be taken very seriously.

Suicide warning signs in teenagers and young adults

An alarming and increasing number of teenagers attempt and succeed at suicide. According to the Centers for Disease Control and Prevention (CDC), suicide is the third leading cause of death for 15- to 24-year-olds. For the overwhelming majority of suicidal teens, depression or another psychological disorder plays a primary role. In depressed teens who also abuse alcohol or drugs, the risk of suicide is even greater.

Because of the very real danger of suicide, teenagers who are depressed should be watched closely for any signs of suicidal thoughts or behavior. The warning signs include:

- Talking or joking about committing suicide.
- Saying things like, "I'd be better off dead," "I wish I could disappear forever," or "There's no way out."
- Speaking positively about death or romanticizing dying ("If I died, people might love me more.")
- Writing stories and poems about death, dying, or suicide.
- Engaging in reckless behavior or having a lot of accidents resulting in injury.
- Giving away prized possessions.
- Saying goodbye to friends and family as if for good.
- Seeking out weapons, pills, or other ways to kill themselves.

If you suspect that a teenager you know is suicidal, take immediate action! For 24-hour suicide prevention and support, call the **National Suicide Prevention Lifeline at**

1-800-273-TALK. To learn more about suicide risk factors, warning signs, and what to do in a crisis, see Helpguide's Suicide Prevention: Understanding and Helping a Suicidal Person. Helpguide.org

Helping a depressed teenager or young adult

If you suspect that a teenager in your life is suffering from depression, take action right away. Depression is very damaging when left untreated, so don't wait and hope that the symptoms will go away. Even if you're unsure that depression is the issue, the troublesome behaviors and emotions you're seeing in your teenager are signs of a problem. Whether or not that problem turns out to be depression, it still needs to be addressed - the sooner the better.

Talk to your teen or young adult

The first thing you should do if you suspect depression is to talk to your teen about it. In a loving and non-judgmental way, share your concerns with your teenager. Let him or her know what specific signs of depression you've noticed and why they worry you. Then encourage your child to open up about what he or she is going through. If he or she is reluctant to talk to you, a sibling, family member, trusted friend or counselor may be consulted. Talk therapy is often more effective than drug therapy.

You can teach your child, adolescent, teenager or young adult how to use the C A R R Y Technique. This helps them to know that God cares about their feelings, concerns and fears. Many of my younger clients use this technique and have reported great success.

IF YOU, YOUR YOUNG PERSON OR ANYONE IS HAVING SUICIDAL OR HOMICIDAL THOUGHTS, HAVE THEM EVALUATED BY A MEDICAL PROFESSIONAL. YOU CAN CALL 911 or TAKE THEM TO THE NEAREST EMERGENCY ROOM.

As I stated earlier, for those who are leary of traditional treatments, you can use PRAYER THERAPY as a supplement to any other necessary treatment.

WARNING!!!
Antidepressant medications may increase the risk of suicidal thinking and behavior in some teenagers. All antidepressants are required by the U.S. Food and Drug Administration (FDA) to carry a "black box" warning label about this risk in children and adolescents. In May 2007, the FDA recommended that the warning be expanded to include young adults from ages 18 to 24. The risk of suicide is particularly great during the first one to two months of antidepressant treatment.
Source: FDA

Although there are many factors in mental illness including chemical imbalances, organic diseases, hormonal imbalances, as in post-partum and other forms of depression, which I by no means intend to minimize; I sincerely believe that if we are taught as early on as possible to incorporate therapeutic prayer for our emotional distresses, many mental diseases and disorders can be prevented.

Summary of Chapter Three

My sincere hope is that you are convinced that God's will is to heal people wholly; spirit soul and body. Many debilitating physical illnesses and premature deaths are caused by mental and emotional maladies. I know of many people who just could not 'get over' the pain of sexual abuse, rejection by parents, abortion and more. Jesus came to heal 'all manner of diseases', bruises, afflictions and brokenness. Being born again does not exempt us from emotional traumas, nor does it always automatically bring healing to such. We are not 'faithless' if we admit to God and specific people who can help us that we need healing in a specific area of emotional pain.

Many wounded Christians have gone to their churches for help, only to receive condemnation, lack of compassion and more hurt. Many have been warned not to look for help. People have reported that organizations such as A.A. and N.A. have helped them far more than the churches that they have attended for years.

Please be free! Cry out to Jesus the Healer as blind Bartimaeus and others did. And the very God of peace, sanctify you wholly: and I pray your whole SPIRIT and SOUL and BODY be preserved blameless unto the coming of our Lord, Jesus Christ. PRAYER THERAPY can help you. Some times God heals instantly, sometimes through a process.

CHAPTER FOUR
What is Prayer Therapy?

A basic definition of the word therapy is the treatment of illness and disease. This applies to physical and mental illnesses. There are many common types of therapies or treatments as we know. Drug therapy, surgery, radiation chemical or chemotherapy are common types of therapies used to treat physical illnesses.

Psychotherapy is the treatment of mental or emotional disorders by psychological techniques such as counseling and other methods.

Prayer Therapy is the practice of using prayer therapeutically in a clinical (intensive treatment and learning session) for the purpose of emotional and mental healing and wholeness.

Prayer Therapy engages the person's SOUL (mind, will, and emotions) in a conscience process of TRANSFORMATION; rather than just praying for them to be healed. LUKE 4:18 ROMANS 12: 2 I THESS.5:23

Prayer Therapy is NOT deliverance in the common usage of the word, although deliverance (freedom from demonic oppression and affliction), will occur. It is our observation that 'deliverance' is relatively easy; but if the affliction is not healed and the mind renewed, the condition will often re-occur, in a relatively short time.

ANALOGY: If you do not know how to ride a bicycle, and you get on and fall off, breaking your arm; I can take the bike away from you but I should also help you to get treatment and healing for your broken arm. If you want to continue riding the bike, I should also teach you how to do it safely and properly.

Similarly, I can pray for God to take away the demonic oppression (deliverance) but I also need to pray for Him to heal your broken heart (an open door for demonic oppression) and I also need to teach you Scripturally based truths and techniques to help you to continue to walk in emotional wholeness. This is the core essence of prayer therapy.

HOW I USED PRAYER THERAPY TO HELP MOLLIE OVERCOME YEARS OF MOLESTATION

First of all, Mollie thought she was okay. She had learned to live with her past pains and since they were hidden, no one could see them. She did not come to see me because of her past traumas. She came to see me because she was in the process of making some important life decisions.

During the first session, Mollie revealed that one of the

decisions that she was making was to move out of the state in order to get away from a bad relationship that she had trouble saying no to. She told me that there was a person in her life that she could not say no to in any way if she saw his face.

You may or may not be able to make a connection between being molested and not being able to say NO especially to sexual advances; but it is common among people who were molested during childhood. They often become promiscuous, for a number of reasons related to the molestation, one of these being they actually feel powerless to assert their will. Yes, although they may be 25 years old now, they were violated against their will at an age when their perpetrator was more powerful physically and mentally. When the perpetrator is a parent or other adult, the confusion is deeper, because by and large children are taught to obey their parents and other adult authority figures.

After several sessions in which we dealt with the molestation problem, Mollie received help for many other behavioral problems that were related to the molestations.

Unfortunately dangerous, mind altering, psychotropic, 'prescription drugs' are being doled out by the millions to people. DRUGS ONLY ALLIEVIATE SYMPTOMS; OFTEN WITH DANGEROUS SIDE EFFECTS THAT ARE MORE SEVERE THAN THE ORIGINAL COMPLAINT.

Even after taking dangerous drugs, if you've had a traumatic experience, it still needs to be healed. It wounded you emotionally. It is just as real as a physical wound. Our emotional wounds, though not visible, need care and attention just the same. If they are not attended, they cause 'infections of the soul'. PRAYER THERAPY can change that.

I can recall two cases that were especially challenging, but the power of prayer, coupled with sensitive caring counseling therapy proved especially beneficial. One was a young man, Carl, who was practicing homosexuality and wanted to stop. He was living with his homosexual partner. He would come to his counseling sessions wearing short-shorts, girlie blouses, and feminine belts. Because I am a Christian Therapist, I could tell that he expected me to insist that he move out of his living situation and make certain outward behavioral changes immediately. I did no such thing. I began to ask him about incidences that made him feel hurt and rejected when he was a child. Subsequent sessions revealed a loveless childhood; an aloof mother, an alcoholic father, and molestation by an older uncle. For weeks I never once addressed his homosexuality.

After using PRAYER THERAPY to bring God's healing love and forgiveness to his pain, he began to change his outward behavior. One day Carl came to his session wearing men's jeans, a shirt and a wide, leather, very masculine belt. He said "look at what I instinctively picked to wear today!" He proceeded to tell me that during the prior several days he had begun to feel untangled from the inside. Instead of feeling like his mind and emotions were confused, he felt 'straight' inside! Interesting.

Without me telling him to, he moved in with a relative in a different city and discontinued the homosexual relationship. A similar situation occurred with middle aged Frank who was an alcoholic. For several weeks he always came to his sessions with the smell of alcohol on his breath. I never mentioned it.

I continued to use PRAYER THERAPY to bring validation to his soul and healing to the pain of rejection and abandonment. One day, he came in; his breath reeked of alcohol as usual. We completed his session. I said to him, Frank, alcohol has been your crutch, you can walk now. He cried like a baby. He continued his sessions with such happiness and freedom. I never smelled alcohol on his breath again. His depression also subsided, and he went on to engage in a productive life.

I have witnessed the power of prayer arrest a woman who was in a paranoid psychotic crisis. She went from 'insanity' to sane within minutes. I saw her every year for several years after. (She lives in a different state than I). She continued to thrive. Once I prayed for a young man at one of my "Second Wind Events." His mother had heard the announcement on the radio. I noticed him because he was very withdrawn; he looked potentially aggressive and kind of 'out of it'. I prayed for him at the end of the meeting. To my utter amazement, he stood up, shook himself as if awakening from a deep sleep, looked around and began to smile and relate to his mother and others around him in a most normal manner. PRAYER THERAPY works for emotional and mental healing as well as for physical healing. I have helped people who were suffering from depression, post traumatic stress syndrome, post abortion syndrome, rejection, abuses of all kind, domestic violence, the gamut. It works, and except in severe cases, individuals can use it by themselves.

From a clinical perspective, PRAYER THERAPY is most effective when applied in cases where the person can participate in the therapeutic process. In the case of Psychoses, PRAYER THERAPY is limited to the practitioner simply praying for the client, similar to how I prayed for the two individuals just mentioned. The long-term results may not be the same unless a follow-up program is implemented.

I am writing this book as a SUPPLEMENT to what you may already be doing, but you need more. The Holy Spirit administers GIFTS of HEALINGS. Many times when God gives someone a revelation, they share it to the exclusion of many of the other great truths that He has revealed for the aid of mankind over the years. ONE REVELATION DOES NOT NEGATE ANOTHER. If a revelation rings true to your spirit and is consistent with the Word and Principles of Scriptures, then ADD it to the knowledge you already have. Just as we need a variety of foods to have a healthy physical body; so there are a number of different virtues that we need to employ to be spiritually and emotionally whole. God is unfolding many truths to help this troubled generation.

Even The Church community and the secular community need to share knowledge and information without each negating the validity of the other. There is nothing spiritual or unspiritual about the invention of the telephone, or the computer, for example. The discrepancies come with use and application, for which every person will answer to God for their own behavior; but many inventions and discoveries are for the benefit of mankind. If it is truth it came from God, regardless to who discovered it. We can embrace knowledge and truth without subscribing to a person's philosophy.

I am passionate about emotional healing because God has instructed me to admonish the body of Christ to not neglect this virtue that is so desperately needed in these times. This does not mean that I am saying we should do away with confession of the Word, Evangelism, Preaching, Deliverance, Breaking generational curses, Spiritual Warfare, Study of the Word, Fasting or any other profitable practice. We need it all! I counseled one lady who has been through both secular and Christian rehab, as well as Deliverance. When I shared the premise of PRAYER THERAPY with her she said, "This is the missing link." Because so many people are suffering due to emotional hurts and traumas, and because Jesus came to 'heal those broken hearts', by the Holy Spirit's direction, I am appealing to us to ADD this virtue to our ministries and to our own lives; to teach it to our children and teenagers. Most of the major hurts and traumas occur during childhood when perceptions are being formed and the psyche is most vulnerable.

I feel that this message is at the CORE of why I was born. God placed me in this wounded generation and gave me this assignment. By writing it, many may benefit long after I have gone home to be with my blessed Savior. Through communicating this message, and encouraging people to KNOW Him as Savior, Deliverer Baptizer in the Holy Spirit, Healer of the brokenhearted and more... I know that I am fulfilling my purpose and destiny. The apostle Peter says it better in II Peter 1:2-15.

"Grace and peace be multiplied unto you through the knowledge of God, and of Jesus our Lord. According as His divine power hath given unto us all things that pertain unto life and godliness, through the knowledge of Him that hath called us to glory and virtue: whereby are given unto us exceeding great and precious promises: that by these ye might be partakers of the divine nature, having escaped the corruption that is in the world through lust. And beside this, giving all diligence, ADD to your faith virtue; and to virtue knowledge; and to knowledge temperance; and to temperance patience; and to patience Godliness; and to Godliness brotherly kindness; and to brotherly kindness charity.
For if these things be in you and abound, they make you that you should neither be barren nor unfruitful in the knowledge of our Lord, Jesus Christ. But he that lacketh these things is blind, and cannot see afar off, and hath forgotten that he was purged from old sins. Wherefore the rather brethren, give diligence to make your calling and election sure: for if ye do these things, ye shall never fall: For so an entrance shall be ministered unto you abundantly into the everlasting kingdom of our Lord and Savior Jesus Christ. Wherefore I will not be negligent to put you always in remembrance of these things, though ye know them, and be established in the present truth. Yea, I think it meet, as long as I am in this tabernacle, to STIR you up by putting

you in rememberance; knowing that shortly I must put off this my tabernacle, even as our Lord Jesus Christ hath shown me. Moreover I will endeavour that ye may able after my decease to have these things always in remembrance."

It will bless you tremendously to study key words in this portion of scripture. It is rich with the process of growth, that we so often want to bypass; yet we want to insist on the blessings of God. This book is also a call to RESPONSIBILITY. God and His promises are NOT A VENDING MACHINE. The apostle Paul said that we are to 'work out' our soul salvation, with fear and trembling. In addition to regular church attendance; study, pray, get to know God through intimate worship, praise and fellowship, apply the knowledge he supplies to you and go on to fulfill destiny.

Some people reading this book have been on a mental, spiritual and emotional merry-go-round for years. We cannot force God to do things the way we think we understand. Be honest, use good sense, dig a little deeper. God says, "call unto me, and I will answer you and show you great and mighty things that thou knowest not." (Jeremiah 33:3 (KJV).

Many people have lost their sanity, departed from the faith, become bitter and angry at God and some have 'died before their time' insisting on trying to get God to do what they want, the way they want; instead of humbly asking God to reveal His specific will in a specific situation and praying in agreement with His will. What a travesty of pride and lack of wisdom.

The Apostle James tells us if we lack wisdom to ask God, he will not chide or ridicule us. When we answer to God, it will be inexcusable and unacceptable to say "well this preacher or this pastor said…" Thank God for Pastors, Teachers, Apostles, Prophets and Evangelists; but in these last days God has sent His Son Jesus Christ, and has also sent the Holy Spirit who is our ultimate teacher. We are personally required to search the scriptures to discern the accuracy and validity of any man or woman's teaching, preaching or prophecy. (See Acts 17:11). One of the Holy Spirit's gifts is DISCERNMENT OF SPIRITS, another is WISDOM. I am learning how incredibly essential it is to ask for both. Our lives on earth and how we serve God is ultimately OUR OWN RESPONSIBILITY.

Summary of Chapter Four

Deliverance may be instantaneous, healing may be instantaneous but TRANSFORMATION is a PROCESS that takes TIME, coupled with GOAL ORIENTED DAILY decisions and corresponding ACTION.

The Bible refers to it as 'working out' your soul salvation. Unhealed Pastors and leaders are hurting their families, entire congregations and beyond; unhealed men and women are hurting each other and their families; the children are being devastated.

Some continue hurting because they don't know how to be healed. Others are hurting because of a condition that I call P.D.D. (PRIDE, DECEPTION and DENIAL).

CHAPTER FIVE
Prayer Therapy vs. Psychotherapy?

I am not a traditional Psychologist. I classify myself as a Counselor/Therapist who takes a holistic approach to therapy; treating the whole person, spirit, soul and body. Much of my educational background is in Communications. (A.A. B.A. B.A. M.A.). This gave me a good overview of the study of Human Behavior. Additionally, I earned a Ph.D. in Psychology and Human Relations and an LHD in Humanities, as it relates to Human thought Processes. It is under the California BP Code that I can legally provide counseling, as an ordained Minister. I am also a Speech Communications Professor. I also studied Christian Counseling while in Bible School; HOWEVER, it is by Divine Mandate that the Lord gave me the Ministry of Emotional Healing in 1983, and told me that His Body needs it. It is primarily the Holy Spirit Who has taught me, and continues to teach me, how to bring His wonderful Healing touch to both individuals, couples and the masses. The need is great.

In chapter one, I define PRAYER THERAPY as the practice of using prayer therapeutically in a clinical (intensive treatment and learning session), for the purpose of emotional and mental healing and wholeness.

Webster's Dictionary in basic terminology defines Psychotherapy as treatment for a mental or emotional disorder. In "Current Psychotherapies" by Raymond Corsins and Danny Wedding, the authors say, "Psychotherapy cannot be defined with any precision." A definition might go as follows:

"Psychotherapy is a formal process of interaction between two parties, each party usually consisting of one person but with the possibility that there may be two or more people in each party, for the purpose of amelioration of distress in one of the two parties relative to any or all of the following areas of disability or malfunction: cognitive functions(disorders of thinking), affective functions (suffering or emotional discomforts), or behavior functions (inadequacy of behavior), with the therapist having some theory of personality's origin, development, maintenance and change along with some method of treatment logically related to the theory and professional and legal approval to act as a therapist."

….And that was all ONE sentence. Now you know why God stepped in (smile).

Jesus simply says, "The Spirit of the Lord is upon me because He hath anointed (empowered and ordained) me to "…heal the broken hearted…" hallelujah!

The entire thesis of this book is "Please allow Him to heal you!"

WHEN THE CHURCH ANATHEMATIZED PSYCHOLOGY WE THREW THE BABY OUT WITH THE BATHWATER

We chuckle at the elaborate definitions of the Psychology scholars because we don't understand the esoteric jargon, but our rejection of the scientific facts of Psychology have cost us. Many of the early "Fathers of Psychology" were students of Sigmund Freud and others who were atheistic in their interpretation and application of Psychology; so the Church in general, rejected all of Psychology. However that was like saying, if an atheist discovered the dynamics that involve the invention of the automobile, we as the Church shall not drive!

The unbiased study of human Behavior, and the documentation of these observations is just pure science. There is nothing religious or non religious about the observation that a child who is deprived of love, affirmation and security often grows up with 'rejection syndrome'. However it is in the application of treatment that the problems with traditional Psychology and the Church occurred. I agree. But does that mean that we ignore the problem? The distress should NOT be ignored or DENIED; nor simply the 'rejection demon' cast out (although this may be necessary also). But we should also minister God's love and His healing touch to that specific area of the child or adult's hurt and pain.

That is what PRAYER THERAPY does and it works. God heals emotional hurts, no matter when they occurred. This is good news, this too is the gospel. Let's teach it, let's preach it, and let's apply it. Similarly, secular Psychology and Psychiatry would do well to learn from those of us who have more expertise in understanding the spiritual component of human composition and other spiritual issues that affect and influence human behavior.

I recently preached a message called "WHAT TO DO WHEN YOU GO THROUGH A PLACE CALLED HELL." Hell as I was referring to it, is a state of misery, extreme discomfort, or torture. As human beings, we go through those experiences and they are not fun to say the least. What we do when we go through those times will make us bitter or better. When we are put in hot water, we can become an egg (hardened, but easy to crack), or a potato, soft, pliable and moldable.

In the Old Testament Book of Jonah, after he has been swallowed by a great fish he said, "I CRIED OUT to the Lord because of my affliction, And He answered me. Out of the belly of Hell I cried, And You heard my voice." The entire second chapter reveals how Jonah 'emoted' his anguish to God and God delivered him.

In Psalm 30: 2 David said, "O Lord God, I CRIED OUT to You and You healed me."

Psalm 66 17-18 says "I CRIED to HIM with my mouth and He was extolled with my tongue. If I regard iniquity in my heart, the Lord will not hear."

Raymond Corsini, one of the authors of "Current Psychotherapies - 5th edition" made the following observation. He says, "Some forty years ago, with a psychiatrist colleague, Dr. Bina Rosenberg, I searched through over 300 articles to identify the critical elements necessary for CHANGING PEOPLE (Corsini & Rosenberg, 1955). We found 220 statements such as "people change when they think that others believe in them" and "the realization that they are not alone makes the difference." We eliminated redundant items and performed a "clinical factor analysis" and identified nine factors.

Cognitive Factors

Universalization: Clients improve when they realize that they are not alone, that others have similar problems, and that human suffering is universal.

Insight: Growth occurs as clients increasingly come to understand themselves and others and gain different perspectives on their own motives and behaviors.

Modeling: People benefit from watching other people. A client may model himself or herself on the therapist.

Affective Factors

Acceptance: This factor reflects the sense of getting unconditional positive regard, especially from the therapist.

Altruism: Change can result from the recognition that one is the recipient of the love and care of the therapist or other members of the group or from being the one who provides love and care to others as well as feeling he is helping others.

Transference: This factor identifies the emotional bond

that occurs between the therapist and the client or between clients in a group setting.

Behavioral Factors
Reality testing: Change becomes possible when clients experiment with new behaviors in the safety of the therapy hour, receiving support and feedback from the therapist and other group members.

Ventilation: This factor encompasses those statements attesting to the value of "blowing off steam" through shouting, crying, or displaying anger in a context in which one could still feel accepted.

Interaction: Clients improve when they are able to openly admit to the group that there is something wrong with themselves or with their behavior.

I believe these nine factors encapsulate the basic mechanisms of therapeutic change. Close examination of this model reveals that the cognitive factors imply "know yourself." The affective factors tell us "Love your neighbor," and the behavioral factor essentially suggests "Do good works." Perhaps there is nothing new under the sun, for this is what philosophers have told us for millennia: "know thyself, love thy neighbor, and do good works."

These are the words of a secular Psychologist. Compare his words with Romans Chapters 12 and 13; I Corinthians

Chapter 13; Matthew 19:19, I Corinthians 10:13 and Ecclesiastes 1:9.

These scriptures speak of being TRANSFORMED by the renewing of your mind; understanding that the tests and trials that you and I face are of the same basic nature that everyone else faces, and to love your neighbor AS you love yourself. This sounds a lot like what some secular psychotherapists are also advocating. In some instances we are just using different terminologies, and as Christians we have the component that makes all the difference. We have the "God-Factor," which enables us to do these things.

Summary of Chapter Five

This chapter advises us to use good sense and discern good from evil as it concerns Psychology and its application. We do not have to discard knowledge, but rather use it for the betterment of man-kind and to the glory of God. We may reject certain psychological theories and philosophies, but we must not fail to bring God's healing to people who are suffering from mental and emotional pains and traumas.

CHAPTER SIX
PRELUDE TO PRAYER THERAPY
Seven Days Toward Emotional Wholeness

Legendary Singer, Natalie Cole, who so graciously wrote the foreword for this book, has shared the story of her journey from drug addiction and the degrading life style that she suffered for years as a result of her addictive behavior. Many people admire her strength and the way she recovered her life and her amazing career. She now enjoys the rewards of incredible success. Her dignity and beauty are intact.

People admire Ms. Cole, but many will not do what she did. She went through the PROCESS of healing and learning how to continue a healthy life-style. I certainly believe in MIRACLES, and have seen many in my life time; however, we have been given a responsibility by God to take care of the lives that he has given us. I have seen occasional instaneous emotional healings, but the majority of the time, the person is required to walk through and participate in the healing process. If all emotional healing were instantaneous, how could one learn how to avoid emotional traumas in the future? If we are not educated during the healing process, we will repeat the same behaviors, which will cause repeated pain. This is what PRAYER THERAPY does. Both the immediate and the long-term results are exceptional.

Prayer therapy does not arbitrarily 'dredge up' issues of the past; quite the contrary. Issues of the past come oozing to the surface one way or another, Prayer Therapy allows the Holy Spirit to reveal the root cause and bring lasting healing and freedom.

Not every bizarre behavior is cause for 'casting out a Demon'. It takes the Holy Spirit's help to discern when a person is suffering from emotional trauma or when they are demonically oppressed or possessed.

I was conducting a woman's retreat once. As I was ministering, the Holy Spirit revealed to me that the Lord was ready to heal people who had been molested and raped, especially those who had held onto the pain of that devastation for 10, 20, 30, one lady even fifty years. They had never told any one. Almost instantly a woman fell to the floor. She began holding her stomach and crying out uncontrollably. "I hate him! I hate him! I hate him!." She was out of control, but it was not demonic. God had created a setting whereby she could be healed and set free. She was!

I call these type meetings, Second Wind Events™. They are often occasions for God to begin miraculous emotional and mental healing. That is when I prescribe a follow-up plan to continue the process. "PRAYER THERAPY: A DAILY PRESCRIPTION" (formerly published as "PRAY THROUGH THE BIBLE IN A YEAR") was written specifically to provide a healthy, therapeutic, daily dose of God's healing word and prayer, 365 days a year. A 21 day supply from that book is provided at the end of this book.

True and lasting emotional healing can only occur when we have deliberate, personal, intimate honest fellowship and communication with God.

Each of these words was chosen carefully. Deliberate means that we set aside a time and place to intentionally communicate with God about our emotional hurts and traumas.

Personal means that it's between us and God (although someone else may assist in the process).

Intimate means we allow God to get really close to us, and we draw really close to Him in our personal time with Him, in addition to our regular church attendance. Tell Him the truth about what has happened to you, how you felt at the time of the event, how it affects you and how you feel now, and humbly ask Him to help you.

Are you ready to begin? Let's begin our first exercise. For the next SEVEN days I invite you to allow the Holy Spirit to take you on a journey TOWARD EMOTIONAL WHOLENESS. This first exercise is NOT for deep emotional pains and traumas. This will mark the beginning of your wonderful journey toward emotional wholeness and freedom; and ultimately move you forward in fulfilling your purpose and destiny on the earth. This is just the beginning.

In order to begin, you need to designate a 'quiet spot' or 'secret place' where you will not be disturbed. (Read Psalm

91). You will need 1. A note book and pen 2. A Bible. Some people have to do this in their car. Begin with at least 30 minutes a day.

This exercise is to get you used to 'emoting' your feeling to God without feeling guilty, or feeling that you don't have faith. Remember blind Bartimaeus "cried out" in spite of criticism from the crowd. He humbly asked Jesus to grant him his sight. Jesus said "your FAITH has made you whole." He exercised his faith by asking Jesus to heal him. This is the same thing that you will be doing; only it will be for an emotional need.

1st DAY

Go to your 'secret place'

Take 15 minutes and admit at least 3 experiences of affliction or hurt to God. At this point, it is better to not write down very devastating experiences. We will address those later. Try to limit these to incidences of offenses, disappointments, hurt feelings etc. Try not to get emotional. Simply write them down. Examples: A friend borrowed money from you, and is now avoiding you, someone gossiped about you, a spouse spoke rudely to you etc.

1.

2.

3.

2nd DAY

Go to your 'secret place'.

1. Spend at least 5 minutes praising and worshipping God. (If you have a prayer language, pray in the spirit).

Ask the Holy Spirit to reveal to you which area(s) of pain (from you first day list) that, you should pray about today.
Pray in the spirit, then in the understanding.
Ask God to heal you in the specific area (s) of pain.
Write your thoughts below:

3rd DAY

Go to your 'secret place'

1. Repeat Day TWO.

2. Verbally (aloud) admit to God that this experience(s) hurt you.

3. Below, tell God how you FEEL about the experience(s). For example, "when my friend betrayed me, I felt hurt, angry disappointed" etc. Emote your feelings thoroughly.

4. Read aloud the entire book of Ephesians.

4th DAY

Go to your 'secret place'

1. Spend at least 5 minutes in praise and worship.
2. Tell God about a different hurtful experience

3. Ask God to heal you from that specific hurt.

a. Read Psalms 139 (aloud).

b. Write out your feelings.

5th DAY

Go to your 'secret place'

1. Write out ways in which you feel that God has disappointed you or not met your expectations or hopes. (be honest with yourself and God).

2. Pray as Hannah did in I Samuel 1:11 (asking God for the thing that you most desire). This time ask Him to be glorified in the answer. Try to trust Him again.

6th DAY

Go to your 'secret place'

1. Spend 5 minutes worshipping and praising God, thanking

Him for every promise, purpose and provision for you.

2. Join Hannah and read her praise aloud.
I Samuel 2: 1-8.

3. Don't ask God for anything today, just praise and worship Him.
4. Write out your thoughts.

7th DAY

Go to your 'secret place'

1. Spend a few minutes praising and worshiping God.

2. Pray, asking God's blessings over the 7 categories of your life. (chapter two).

3. Pray Hannah's prayer in I Samuel Chapter 2 vss. 1-10.

Write your thoughts freely on your journal page.

You should have experienced some degree of 'freedom' and lessening of oppression by now.

These exercises are to prepare you in using my CARRY technique for deeper hurts and pains.

Summary of Chapter Six

Hopefully you did the exercises, or at least read through

them and intend to go back and do them later. That's fine. The goal is to simply encourage you to allow God, The Holy Spirit to be your Counselor, and Jesus Christ to be your Healer for emotional pain. Soon your 'secret place' will be anywhere that you are; the idea is to make God your 'secret place' and refuge as stated in Psalm 91.

David said in Ps. 51:6 "Behold, you desire truth in the inward parts, And in the hidden part You will make me to know wisdom." In other words if we are honest and truthful with God about how we really feel inside, He will often show us, why we are hurting, how to be healed, and how to handle hurts in the future so that no 'root of bitterness' will spring up in our lives. This only happens in deliberate, personal, intimate, honest, fellowship and communication with God and His Son, Jesus Christ. His name is Wonderful, Counselor, Mighty God, and The Prince of Peace!

CHAPTER SEVEN
Dr. Minnie Claiborne's C-A-R-R-Y Technique

I promised to share with you a PRAYER THERAPY EXERCISE using my original technique which I call the C-A-R-R-Y technique. It is a 5-segmented prayer that can effectively assist you in your journey toward emotional wholeness. I have proven this technique with countless clients, and I continue to use it in my personal life.

This you will also do in your 'QUIET SPOT' OR YOUR 'SECRET PLACE'. You can make yourself an appointment once a week or as often as you desire. If you are serious, and want to learn how to be emotionally healed and how to remain healed this may be the most important technique that you will ever learn. It is fairly basic and simple, but it works!

You can do this exercise alone or with someone who you trust completely. If you are too distressed, or feel that a hurt or experience is too painful to do without professional help, do not attempt to do it.

Although the C-A-R-R-Y technique may seem simple, be sure to go through all 5 steps each time you do your sessions.

I will explain, in simple terms, what the five steps are, then give you an example of how to use them. You will learn to use this technique very quickly and you'll be surprised how many times you will have an opportunity to use it in a given day. It's amazing how many little mental and emotional bruises and hurts we 'carry' around. Imagine how many times we are hurt over the years, and we just keep living with the pains, big and small. Here is a technique that you can use throughout your lifetime.

Before you begin, be sure to read the directions thoroughly until you are sure that you understand them. The word C-A-R-R-Y is an acrostic, each letter stands for a word that tells you how to complete that segment of the prayer. Don't do the exercise yet, just read the following for understanding.

C ~ CRY OUT- This is the first part of your 5-part prayer. In this segment you will simply verbalize to God. Tell Him what and who hurt you, and how you feel. You are doing what Jonah, David and Blind Bartimaeus did.

EXAMPLE: Dear God, I am bringing before you the incident that happened at work today. My boss embarrassed me again, in front of my co-workers. He/She made me feel inadequate, embarrassed, incompetent and angry. I wanted to walk out and never look back. I feel so hurt, angry and so frustrated. (Emote thoroughly).

A ~ASK- In the second segment of the prayer, petition or ask God's intervention, BE SURE TO ASK HIM TO HEAL ANY HURT FEELINGS THAT OCCURRED IN YOU.

EXAMPLE: Lord, I ask you for the power to forgive my

boss, as an act of my will. I ask you for wisdom and your solution to this problem. I ask you to heal my emotions and take away the hurt, anger, frustration and feelings of revenge. I ask you to intervene in the situation and work it out for my good and your glory. In Jesus name, Amen.

R - RECEIVE- In the third segment of the prayer, tell God that by faith in Him and His word, you believe and receive the answer to the prayer that you just prayed.

EXAMPLE: Dear God, I thank you that your word assures me that you hear me when I pray. (quote appropriate scriptures as you desire). I receive your power to forgive, I receive healing for the hurt I experienced, and I receive deliverance from anger and feelings of revenge. In the name of Jesus Christ, Amen.

You should feel better by now, but…..be sure to KEEP GOING! PRAY IT ALL THE WAY THROUGH EACH TIME!

R - RELEASE- This is where your faith comes in. Imagine that you have just given your case (your situation) to the master attorney of the universe. Stand up and begin walking and make throwing gestures with your hands. Make a declaration such as this;
"Lord, I cast this care completely upon You. You alone are able to vindicate me, You are my provider, my redeemer. I give the case to You, and I know that You are already working it out. (do this as long and as thoroughly as you need to).

Y – YIELD – Lean toward God through praise, worship and thanksgiving. His peace and joy and assurance will begin to minister to your soul. Note: Often one incident of hurt or rejection etc. may stir up 'old emotional injuries' that never healed. If this occurs, great: use the CARRY Technique to bring healing to those also. Perhaps God allowed them to come to mind now because you have an additional resource to assist you in your healing.

NOTE: You may not immediately know WHY you are hurting inside. Do the CARRY Technique with the 'unknown' ailment, and follow it through, asking God to heal you, and if He chooses, to reveal to you anything else you need to know about the situation. Some things may not be necessary for you to know in detail. Praise God for His great wisdom.

Remember the words to this timeless hymnal:

"What a friend we have in Jesus,
All our sins and grief's to bear.
What a privilege to C-A-R-R-Y
Everything to God in prayer.

Oh what peace we often forfeit,
Oh what needless pain we bear,
All because we do not C-A-R-R-Y
EVERYTHING to God in prayer."

The C A R R Y Technique works best when you address specific incidences, rather than generalizing a situation. This validates the repressed feelings of hurt, anger, frustration, and the ungrieved griefs. For example, you may say "when my mother died I felt alone and frightened." This is a good starting point, but you may need to also pray about specific incidences, such as the exact moment when you received the news or saw her take her last breath.

Here is a list of the kinds of experiences that respond when using the C A R R Y Technique:

ABUSES- Sexual, mental, emotional and physical; including molestation, rape, incest, sodomy, oral rape, date rape and spousal rape, physical abuse

Abandonment or perceived abandonment

Love or affection withheld from you

Mental Torment

Abortion

Adoption

Anger

Betrayal

Death

Divorce

Fear

Discrimination

Verbal Abuse

Domestic Violence Hotline: 1 800-799-S A F E

Rejection

Various Traumas

CAUTION: If you have especially painful, devastating situations, DO NOT DO THIS ALONE. Consult a mental health professional who believes in using prayer in the therapeutic process. In incidences that are serious, but not as devastating, you may choose to enlist the assistance of a mature, close friend; someone with whom you feel completely comfortable, and who will not fall apart as you are emoting, but can serve as a sensitive coach to help you to pray all the way through to victory and healing.

In many instances, "deliverance" from the demonic aspect of certain afflictions must occur in order for healing to be complete. Often you can bind and loose these yourself. You may need to PRAYERFULLY seek the ministry of someone with a stronger anointing. Be aware of 'quick fixes'. Deliverance does NOT negate the need for emotional healing. You can shue a fly away from an open sore, but as long as the wound is exposed, the fly will return. I highly recommend "Binding the Strong Man" and other books by Archbishop N. Duncan-Williams and The "Rules of Engagement" series by

Dr. N. Cindy Trimm as complements to PRAYER THERAPY. The more thoroughly you emote and petition, the more effective the exercise. You may feel self-conscious at first, but if you continue you will soon feel comfortable and the benefits will be life-changing. Soft, non-distracting anointed music will help to set the proper atmosphere.

I suggest you first use the technique on an incident that is not extremely painful, but that is serious enough for you to gage it's effectiveness. An uncomfortable encounter with a co-worker or family is a good example.

Here is how a lady named Carolyn used the C A R R Y technique. Carolyn's mother-in-law takes every opportunity to make her feel inadequate and unworthy of her only son. After Carolyn invited her in-laws over for a steak dinner one night; her mother-in-law said,(within Carolyn's hearing) "I'll need a couple of spools of dental floss after that!" Carolyn used the CARRY Technique to pray about her hurt feelings and not allow the incident to weigh on her and cause her to become depressed or bitter. This is how she prayed.

Heavenly Father, my mother-in-law insulted me again! I feel hurt, angry, and embarrassed and frustrated. I am tired of trying to win her approval. I'm also angry at my husband for not putting a stop to this. I feel disgusted by her insults, and appalled by her audacity. I am fed-up!

I ask you to please let your forgiveness flow through me to her. I ask you to please heal this hurt and take away the anger and frustration. Give me wisdom in this situation, so that I may maintain my joy and peace. I bind the spirits of division that are aimed at my husband and I ask for unity and oneness and your divine solution to this problem, in Jesus' name. Father God, I receive everything that I have just asked for. Your word tells me that this is the confidence that I have in you that you hear and answer me when I pray. I now release this entire situation into your able hands; trusting that You will perfect everything that concerns me. I know that You are able to do exceedingly abundantly above all that I can ask or think. I worship and praise you. You are the only wise God. Praise Your name forevermore, Amen.

You may choose to do PRAYER THERAPY once a week for serious issues. Do it as the Holy Spirit leads you.

For maximum effectiveness, remember to set aside AT LEAST thirty minutes to an hour in your 'quiet spot' so that you can reap the full benefits of this time. You are actually making a counseling appointment with the Holy Spirit. He will meet you there. He is your Helper.

Many people find it helpful to have soft worship music (instrumental may be more appropriate). Invite the Holy Spirit in and begin to worship.

In Chapters One and Two, I talk about the seven secrets in the garden. The first one embraces the realization that as human beings, we are comprised of SPIRIT, SOUL and BODY. PRAYER THERAPY engages your spirit and encourages you to develop a relationship with God who is also a SPIRIT. The Bible tells us that our human spirits are dis-connected from God until we have an experience that connects our spirits to God.

It is called being 'born again' or saved.

You will never receive the FULL benefits of PRAYER THERAPY until you humbly accept the truth that as wonderful and as intelligent and as beautiful or as handsome, how rich or how poor you are, you need access to a power greater than yourself and greater than any human being in order to deal with certain issues in your life. That is precisely one of the reasons God sent us a Savior to earth, His name is Jesus Christ. It is our (missing the mark, SINS) that prevent us from connecting to God. We were born with the disease of sin. The Bible tells us that Jesus Christ is the cure for that sin, if we receive Him. Medicine can only cure an ailment if you take it.

Here is the first step:
Pray-talk to God sincerely. Your prayer may go something like this:

Dear God,
I need a Savior, I want to be connected to you. The sickness of sin is destroying my life. I need you. I invite your Son, Jesus Christ to come into my life, to forgive all of my sins, and to be my Lord and Savior. Jesus, I accept you as my Lord and Savior, come in and begin to lead me, guide me teach me, heal me help me. Fill me with the Holy Spirit and empower me for abundant life and good success. John 3:16, Acts 4:12, Romans 10.

You will need to pray for God to lead you to a good church, you will need to be baptized and begin studying the scriptures. A 21-Day Prescription of BIBLE STUDY and PRAYER THERAPY is included at the end of this book. My book,

READ AND PRAY THROUGH THE BIBLE contains 365 days of Prayers. You may order it online at WWW.DRMINNIE.NET.

Here is the CARRY TECHNIQUE for quick reference.

C Cry-Out - Tell God the situation and emote your feelings thoroughly.

A Ask - Petition God exhaustively concerning the situation.

R Receive - Affirm that you receive God's help and intervention.

R Release – Fully verbalize and mentally release the situation to God.

Y Yield - Yield to God in praise, worship and thanksgiving. Be still and experience His presence. Write on your Journal page.

CHAPTER EIGHT
A 21 Day Prescription of Prayer Therapy

In order to maintain the healing that you obtain in your prayer therapy time, you will need to take your DAILY PRESCRIPTION. I have included a 21 Day supply in the following pages. At the back of the book, space is provided for journaling so that you can write your insights for later review and reflection.

RECOMMENDED DOSAGE: I recommend that you read the synopsis and pray the prayer daily. It is important that you DELIBERATELY set aside time, even if its 5 minutes a day; mornings are best as this will give you food for thought and meditation throughout the day, but don't be too rigid.

Choose a different time during the day, or expand your devotion time to read the scripture references in your own Bible. By doing this, you can both READ and PRAY through the Scriptures. IF you continue with your MONTHLY PRESCRIPTIONS, you will have READ and PRAYED through the entire Bible. If you do this sincerely, and with concentration and focus, your life will definitely be abundantly blessed and transformed.

Do not just read the daily prayers. Be sure to PRAY the prayers with concentration, reflection and sincerity.

A 21 DAY PRESCRIPTION of PRAYER THERAPY

DAY ONE: Genesis 1-2

In Genesis chapters one and two, we see the Almighty God as Creator of the Heavens, the earth, and all living things, including the human race. God establishes order and purpose out of chaos. He also establishes the fact that males and females are created in His image; and are given provision as well as dominion and responsibility.

PRAYER
Dear Heavenly Father, Creator of the Heavens and the earth, I honor you also as the one who made me in your image and likeness. Dear God in places or at points in my life where there is confusion and darkness, I pray Let there be the light of your wisdom and counsel. Where there is chaos in my spirit, soul, body or relationships, please bring your divine order.

Where I have lacked purpose, remind me that I was created by you with a divine destiny and a specific purpose. I pray that you will provide me with whatever I need in order to take my responsibility and fulfill your great purpose in my life.

I pray for forgiveness for the times that I have tried to be in control of my own life. I now submit to you, and your plans Heavenly Father, in the name of Jesus Christ, Amen.

TODAY'S CHALLENGE:
May I know that God has the wisdom and the ability to direct every aspect of my life perfectly.

What else is God saying to me today?

What is my response?

DAY TWO: Genesis 3-5

In these verses the tempter, the serpent, enters the scene with the sole purpose of usurping God's word, and tempting man, God's highest creation, to sin against God and nullify His purposes and blessings in their lives. The cunning serpent challenges the word of God. The woman and man eat of the forbidden tree, disobeying God, and bringing judgment on themselves and the entire human race. Intimate fellowship with God is replaced with fear, shame and curses. The evidence of Adam and Eve's sin culminates in deception, jealousy and murder through their firstborn son, Cain. However because of God's great love, we also see redemption on the horizon through their son Seth and grandson Enosh.

PRAYER
Most Holy, awesome God,
Please help me to never doubt or compromise your word, or be a victim of satanic deception or manipulation which will lead me to disobey you. Please forgive my sins and those of your erring children. Help me to never evoke curses upon myself or my family through willful sin and disobedience.

Please remove the curse of sin that I have inherited or initiated. May all such curses be removed from me and my family through every generation; past, present and future. Let the restoration that comes by calling upon your name be evident and active in my life and in the lives of my family members. In the name of Jesus Christ, I pray.

TODAY'S CHALLENGE:

Lord help me to know that the truth of your word planted in my heart and spoken through my mouth is able to pierce through generational sins and produce a harvest of blessings.

What else is God saying to me today?

What is my response?

DAY THREE: Genesis 6-9

As mankind continues to multiply upon the earth, sin's legacy continues to the point that God decides to destroy his own creation. How this must have grieved the heart of God. In His mercy, God spares Noah and his family, thus preserving mankind, with the purpose of continuing his redemptive plan. He makes a covenant with Noah and his sons and reiterates the original command, "Be fruitful and multiply."

PRAYER
My Dear God,
please forgive me and all of your people for choosing to sin and for grieving your heart. What wickedness we have brought upon the beautiful earth that you created for us to enjoy.
Help me to find grace in your eyes. Help me to walk with you and follow all that you command. In the midst of a sin-infested society, help me to be salt and light and obey your word.

After your miraculous deliverances and provisions for me, please help me to not be drunk with the wine of complacency; but alert and sober, so that I can fulfill my responsibilities admirably.

In the name of Jesus Christ, I pray, Amen.

TODAY'S CHALLENGE:

To what extent can I listen to the voices of my world and still hear and obey the voice of my God? Is there an area of compromise that God is challenging me to abandon today?

What else is God saying to me today?

What is my response?

DAY FOUR: Genesis 10-11

The families of the sons of Noah indeed multiply and inhabit the earth; they all speak one language. What an opportunity to unite and worship God the creator, united with one language, in one accord. What glory that would have brought to God, and what blessings to the people.

Instead, we see another of sin's off springs, rebellion. The people begin to unite together to challenge God, and attempt to make a city and a name for themselves. God intervenes so that the people do not destroy themselves through idolatry. He confuses their language and scatters them abroad so that their wicked plans do not succeed.

PRAYER
Dear Heavenly Father,
please reveal to me any areas in my life where I tend to rely upon my genealogy, intellect, ethnicity, money or anything earthly instead of you. I know that reliance upon any of these things is idolatry and rebellion which is sin. Help me to not make unholy alliances simply because of what I might have in common with a person or groups of people. You alone are God, and I choose to honor you above all things and seek your wisdom and counsel each day.

Help me not to attempt to build or make any plans of which you have not approved. Thank you for constantly guiding me back onto the right path so that I will see your precious promises fulfilled in my life.
In the name of Jesus Christ I pray, Amen.

TODAY'S CHALLENGE:

Can I, with my own understanding really accomplish what I think I can and get God results?

What else is God saying to me today?

What is my response?

DAY FIVE: Genesis 12-15

Abram is a key figure in the history of mankind. God chose to reveal himself to and through Abraham with a promise to bless him personally, to bless his descendants, and indeed through him to bless all the families of the earth.

Abram is challenged to leave all that is familiar and dear to him and to simply follow God with only the reward of a promise. "And he believed in the Lord, and He accounted it to him for righteousness." There is a sense of awe as we see evidence of God's commitment by covenant to Abraham, and His faithfulness to His promises in spite of Abram's flaws.

PRAYER
Dear God, Most High, Possessor of Heaven and earth,
may my fellowship with you be so special, so honest and so trusting, that I will have faith to leave the familiar if necessary, in order to follow your wonderful plan.

Help me to be submitted to you in a posture of perpetual worship, so that my life will be an extension of your plan and so that I may be blessed, my descendants may be blessed, and that I may be a blessing to the families of the earth that you may send me to.

May I honor you in worship, in tithes and in faith. Thank you for revealing aspects of your nature to us by allowing the record of your relationship with Abram to be preserved. Please feel free to speak to me, and help me to have a heart that will obey. In the name of Jesus Christ I pray Amen.

TODAY'S CHALLENGE:

What does God's voice sound like?
Do I listen to him often enough to recognize his voice?

What else is God saying to me today?

What is my response?

DAY SIX: Genesis 16-19

Our carnal plans sorely contrast with God's promises. In these chapters we see Sarai and Abram trying to help God's plan along. God had promised them a son. They are both past childbearing age, and the promise has not been fulfilled. Their impatience is understandable. God continues to reiterate His promises to them because He knows that in spite of their detour into carnality, Abraham will perpetuate his faith through his descendants, and the promises of God will be fulfilled. God continues to encourage Abraham and Sarah, even affirming them by changing their names. The men of Sodom are so depraved that they practically tear Lot's house down in order to sleep with two men who are actually angels. God destroys the cities of Sodom and Gomorrah with fire and brimstone. The angels usher Lot and his family out, commanding them to not look back. His wife disobeys and turns into a pillar of salt.

PRAYER
Dear God Almighty,
how faithful you are to your word despite our doubts, anxieties and fears. As you were faithful to Abraham and Sarah in their weakness, please be so to me. Take the mistakes that I have made and use them for your purpose. Help me never to doubt you or your promises. There is nothing too hard for you. I receive from you the faith, patience, perseverance and wisdom to wait for the fulfillment of your promises in my life. Help me to also recognize your presence in my present situations and receive your comfort and counsel. When you want to

destroy the things in my past, help me to not set my affections on them and look back as Lot's wife did. I ask these things in the name of Jesus Christ, Amen.

TODAY'S CHALLENGE:

To REST while I wait on the Lord to fulfill his promises in my life, and in the lives of those who I love and pray for.

What else is God saying to me today?

What is my response?

DAY SEVEN: Genesis 20-22

Evidence of God's incredible grace is constantly revealed in Abraham and Sarah's lives. Out of fear, Abraham is not completely honest with Abimelech; again God intervenes. In the following chapter, Isaac, the long awaited promise is about to be conceived. It's unthinkable to imagine what would have happened if Abimelech's plans for Sarah had been carried out.

God is perfectly arranging every thing in order to fulfill His promises to Abraham and Sarah at just the right time, and in just the right place, for just the right purpose. Meanwhile he is working many miracles while they wait.

What incredible trust and friendship Abraham had with God. His obedience and faith are at their zenith when he proceeds to offer his son of promise as a burnt sacrifice on the altar to God.

PRAYER

Most Holy God, I'm sure I've failed many tests, but I pray to have a pure heart. Please intervene when I am afraid or unsure. As you did with Abraham and Sarah, keep me from hindering the fulfillment of your promises in my life. Help me to remember that you are with me, even when I feel alone.

May your grace, favor and peace preserve me from fear and doubt. May I continually read your word so that I may be reassured of your presence. And Lord, the things that I hold most dear, I offer up to you by faith. Please overshadow my fears with the faith to know that in the hour of my greatest

tests, your miraculous provisions will always manifest.
In the name of Jesus Christ I pray, Amen.

TODAY'S CHALLENGE:

Lord help me to know that one of the smallest words in my language, FAITH, is the biggest key to receiving your greatest promises.

What else is God saying to me today?

What is my response?

DAY EIGHT: Genesis 23-26

Abraham loses his beloved Sarah to death. As is normal, he mourns the wife that he loved. He secures a burial place for her. God had expressed confidence that Abraham would command his descendents in the way of the Lord. Abraham realizing that he is advanced in age, makes provisions for his son Isaac. He sends his servant out to be divinely led to Rebekah, the woman who will become Isaacs's wife.

Abraham later marries Keturah and has six more sons. As God promised, Abraham blessed all of his sons and sent them to various parts of the earth.
Because of Abraham's obedience to God, the promises of God were passed on to Isaac and his descendants.

PRAYER
Dear Faithful, Loving God,
some of life's experiences are very painful. We see Abraham mourning the death of the love of his life, yet not forgetting to honor you. Please help me to not close you out because of bitter and painful events that have occurred in my life. Abraham's life was not without many trials and tests, but he remained committed to God, and committed to passing the legacy on to his descendants.
In my weaknesses and disappointments help me to see and let others know that you are still a good God. In the name of Jesus Christ, Amen.

TODAY'S CHALLENGE:

Lord help me to experience the reality that my faith's anchor will hold during stormy weather.

What else is God saying to me today?

What is my response?

DAY NINE: Genesis 27-29

In these and the preceding chapters we see the promises of God continuing in spite of imperfect vessels. The promises that God made to Abraham remain in Isaac, and his sons Esau and Jacob. The interesting thing is that both the promises of God and the weaknesses of their humanity are passed from one generation to the next. Isaac fails in the same ways that Abraham did. Both Esau and Jacob fail also; only God's word remains true.

Although God's word remains true, the descendants of Abraham suffered greatly due to their human weaknesses. We can learn from their mistakes, and pray for wisdom.

PRAYER
Dear God,
how we fail in our efforts to find our way in life just like the patriarchs in the Bible. However we have the help of the Holy Spirit and the written word that gives us the ability to analyze their mistakes and pray that we not enter into the same temptations.

O Lord, may we have the faith of Abraham without the failures, the blessings as Isaac without the blindness, the inheritance of your promises as Esau and Jacob, without the deception and greed. In the name of Jesus Christ, Amen.

TODAY'S CHALLENGE:

May my human weaknesses and that of others cause me to draw closer to God who is the only truly reliable refuge.
In what areas of my life am I relying on human strength and wisdom without properly consulting God?

What else is God saying to me today?

What is my response?

DAY TEN: Genesis 30-32

Jacob, whose name means supplanter, is reaping what he has sown. His uncle Laban, treats him the same way he and his mother treated his father Isaac and his brother, Esau. Jacob works hard and is treated poorly by Laban, yet in the midst of his affliction God speaks to him and directs him to go back to the land of his fathers. During his period of suffering, God does not forsake Jacob, but blesses him greatly in spite of his adverse circumstances.
Finally, Jacob has a monumental life-changing encounter with angels. He "wrestles" all night until he receives a blessing from the Lord. At this time God changes his name from Jacob to Israel-from supplanter to prince.

PRAYER
Dear Lord,
these scriptures show the very human side of Jacob. Yet he called out to you for deliverance and you blessed and changed him. I have areas of my life that need to be blessed and changed. I ask you to be gracious to me in areas where I must reap what I have sown.
May I also encounter your very presence in the midst of my struggles.
Please forgive me and change me wherever change is needed, so that I may go wherever you send me without the burden of guilt and fear.
In the name of Jesus Christ, I pray, Amen.

TODAY'S CHALLENGE:

May shame and pride not serve as chains and padlocks to keep me bound.

Is God lovingly asking me to sincerely and earnestly cry out to Him for deliverance?

Am I willing to do it right now?

What else is God saying to me today?

What is my response?

DAY ELEVEN: Genesis Chapters 33-36

God moves on the heart of Esau who had issued a death threat against Jacob 20 years earlier, and the brothers are reconciled.

After much growth, struggle and finally transformation, Jacob enters into his place of promise. As a way of life, we see that upon entering each place of rest, Jacob erects an altar to God first. As Israel, formerly Jacob, makes a habit of honoring God first, God reaffirms his name and reaffirms His promises.

PRAYER
Most Holy God in Heaven,
please let my past sins be forgiven, let there be reconciliation wherever needed, and let me see your vision of who I am and who I am becoming with your help. Thank you lord.
In the name of Jesus Christ, Amen.

TODAY'S CHALLENGE:

May I not struggle to hold on to my behaviors that belie who I am; but to enter into a place of rest in the presence of God; so that he can show me who He has created me to be.

What else is God saying to me today?

What is my response?

DAY TWELVE: Genesis 37-39

Joseph's brothers sin against him because he is favored by his father. They are further infuriated when Joseph shares a dream and vision of being elevated to a position of leadership over them. Moved with jealousy and envy, they stage his death and sell him into slavery.

Despite being a victim of such cruelty, the Bible tells us that the hand of the Lord is upon Joseph so that he finds favor, and is blessed and he prospers wherever he goes. Just when things are going well for Joseph in Egypt, he is wrongly accused and sent to prison; but the Lord's hand is still with him and he finds mercy and favor.

Meanwhile his brother Judah, who is free, acts outside of the will of God and sins with the Canaanites; which begins a chain-reaction of unholy consequences.

PRAYER
Dear Heavenly Father,
Help me to remember that where I am is not as important as who I am and who is with me. Seemingly plagued with misfortune, Joseph still prospered where he was placed and did not compromise his integrity even when no one was watching.

Help me to see that in the most unfortunate situations, as I remain connected to you, and faithful to who you have ordained me to be, you will find a way to bless me. In the name of Jesus Christ, I pray, Amen.

TODAY'S CHALLENGE:

Am I the same person in public that I am when I think that no one sees me?

What else is God saying to me today?

What is my response?

DAY THIRTEEN: Genesis 40-42

In these chapters we see Joseph's gifts emerge. We think that we will see him released because of the promise of his fellow prison mate, the chief butler, but he forgets about speaking to the Pharaoh on Joseph's behalf. Amazingly the Bible does not suggest in any way that Joseph becomes bitter. He accepts his lot, and waits upon the lord.

It is two years later before the opportunity came for Joseph to witness to Pharaoh through the gift that God gave him. Finally God, through Pharaoh, elevates Joseph to the place of destiny where he could do the most good, and God could get the most glory.

Joseph's dream, which was really God's dream has come to pass. Circumstances cause Joseph's brothers to come to Egypt for provisions because of a famine in their country. They bowed down to Joseph. He recognizes them, but he is so blessed of God that the family that sinned against him don't recognize him.

PRAYER
O Lord,
only with your grace and mercy and your hand upon me will I be able to bear such mistreatments as Joseph did without sinning. Perhaps a clearer vision of your dream and destiny for me will help me to be totally focused on your purpose for my life. May that vision so consume me, that I will not be moved by adversities that I encounter. In the name of Jesus Christ, Amen.

TODAY'S CHALLENGE:

May God's presence in me be so comforting and healing, that if someone sins against me and expects to see me full of anger, bitterness and unforgiveness; I will be so full of the love, healing and forgiveness of God that they won't recognize me.

What else is God saying to me today?

What is my response?

DAY FOURTEEN: Genesis 43-46

Although Joseph gave his brothers provisions, the famine was so great that they had to return to Egypt and Joseph for help. Joseph continues to investigate and interrogate them. As Judah intercedes and humbles himself before Joseph, Joseph can no longer constrain his compassion and his longing to see his father.

He reveals himself to his brothers who become speechless with dismay. Joseph comforts and assures them that what they did worked into God's plan to send him to Egypt to be a Savior and deliverer for them.

Because God blessed Joseph, he is able to bless his entire family and be the instrument that God used to secure them in the best land in Egypt with abundant provisions despite the famine throughout their country. Before Israel departs for Egypt he offers sacrifices to God, God reassures him and promises to make him a great nation in Egypt.

PRAYER
Lord God of Abraham, Isaac and Jacob, and my God,
I bow before you in awe. You are the God who makes promises and keeps them, who gives dreams and fulfills them in spite of adversities, delays and human weaknesses.

My faith is refreshed by your word today. I pray again with expectation that in my life too; you will fulfill every God-given dream and promise that work for my good and the good of others, and for your glory.
In the name of Jesus Christ I pray, Amen.

TODAY'S CHALLENGE:

May I offer the sacrifices of praise and worship to my God who is faithful to fulfill his promises to me and make his dreams for me come true.

What else is God saying to me today?

What is my response?

DAY FIFTEEN: Genesis 47-50

Joseph tells Pharaoh about his family, and introduces him to his father, Jacob. Jacob blesses Pharaoh and because of Joseph's faithfulnesses and subsequent promotion; Jacob and his entire family, which by now has grown tremendously, is blessed.

Interestingly, before he dies, Jacob bestows the blessings of the first born of Joseph's sons on the younger. Jacob did not follow tradition, but was led by the Holy Spirit. He prophesies over, and blesses each of his sons; specifying and foretelling that the kingly lineage of the messiah, Jesus Christ will come through the lineage of Judah.

After the death of Jacob, Joseph reassures his brothers that he will not retaliate against them. It is here that we find the immortal phrase: "you meant it for evil, but God meant it for good." Joseph continues to prosper in Egypt until his death.

PRAYER
Dear God, please help me to live my life in such a manner that you will bless me and cause me to be a blessing to others. Joseph is such a clear typification of the Savior, Jesus Christ. His attitude, his life, his ultimate ascension to the right hand of Pharaoh, all point to Christ the Messiah. Thank you for your great and manifold provisions. In the name of Jesus Christ I pray, Amen.

TODAY'S CHALLENGE:

Who do people say I remind them of?

What else is God saying to me today?

What is my response?

DAY SIXTEEN: Job 1-4

In this book, we are introduced to a man Job, who is upright, blameless, fears God and shuns evil. He also has great material possessions.

Suddenly overwhelming calamity befalls Job. He loses his children and all of his possessions in one day. Apparent to us as readers, but not to Job immediately, this is a vicious attack from Satan, with God's permission. A second attack of Satan leaves Job with painful boils on his body from the soles of his feet to the crown of his head. Instead of luxuriating in splendor and grandeur with maid and menservants which his previous wealth could afford him, he now sits in a pile of ashes, scraping himself with a potsherd. At this point his fate looks so eminent that his wife tells him to curse God and die. The Bible says. "In all of this Job does not sin with his lips." He looks so bad that his friends do not recognize him. When they do they weep out loud and sprinkle dust on their heads toward Heaven. Job's grief is so heavy that for seven days and seven nights his friends sit and mourn with him in silence. No one says a word.

Job's wife and friends are completely baffled because according to their understanding of God, good things happen to good people, and bad things happen to bad people. In the words of Job's friend, Eliphaz. "No one perishes if he is not guilty." Job feels such grief that he wishes that he had never been born.

PRAYER
Dear Lord,
Job's calamities seem more than I would ever be able to bear. I know that in my world the attitude of Job's friends and wife are pervasive. "If you're suffering calamity, or having a hard time, there must be sin in your life, there must be something that you're doing wrong." Job's experience illustrates the fact that bad things actually do happen to good people. If ever I am the victim of calamity, help me to not curse you. If ever I am in a position of comforting someone on whom calamity has fallen, please help me not to be smug, suspicious or judgmental; but to show mercy and kindness and to offer prayer to God on their behalf. In Jesus name I pray, Amen.

TODAY'S CHALLENGE:

Some things happen that defy human explanation; at those times, God help me to not try and offer answers, to myself or to anyone else. Help me to just pray.

What else is God saying to me today?

What is my response?

DAY SEVENTEEN: Job 5-7

Eliphaz, one of Job's friends, conjectures that God is disciplining Job, correcting him because he is guilty of something. In his mind it is unfathomable that someone could be upright and suffer such affliction. Eliphaz presents an entire treatise on how God operates, to prove to Job that it is his sin that God is judging.

In anguish, Job prays for God to kill him. He does not understand what is happening to him, and feels like he is a target for God's wrath.

He appeals to his friend for kindness, but his friend only adds to his affliction by undermining and judging him. Job questions God.

PRAYER
Oh Lord, in times of great affliction when I may feel like a target of your wrath; help me to know that I more likely am a target of Satan's wrath, and that you have not forsaken me. Help me to remember that Satan does not have the permission or the freedom to destroy my life. Help me to remain steadfast in the time of trouble.
In the name of Jesus Christ I pray, Amen.

TODAY'S CHALLENGE:

To hold on to my faith in God beyond what my mind can comprehend.

What else is God saying to me today?

What is my response?

DAY EIGHTEEN: Job 8-10

Another of Job's friends, Bildad also questions Job's integrity, and suggests that he is really a hypocrite. Stating that if Job were really upright God would help him.
Job answers reflect his utter frustration. He knows that he is crying out to God, that he did not sin, but feels that he has no recourse to defend himself before his friend or before God.

He questioned the seemingly senselessness of his affliction. He asked questions such as, "Why did you so intricately fashion me only to destroy me?"

PRAYER
Heavenly Father, I don't always understand the things that happen to me or to other people. I can only learn day by day to trust in your goodness and integrity. In the midst of my questions, because of various situations, help me to maintain a sense of your presence by faith if not by sight. Just as I walk into a darkened room and feel my way along the wall until I find the light switch; help me to reach out for your light in the middle of my darkest midnights until I feel your hand sustaining me.

In the name of Jesus Christ, Amen.

TODAY'S CHALLENGE:

May my hope for deliverance be based on God's integrity, not on my own, or my friend's.

What else is God saying to me today?
What is my response?

DAY NINETEEN: Job 11-13

Zophar, another of Job's friends affirm the verdict of the other two. His summation of the situation is that if Job were righteous this evil would not have befallen him and that he should repent. In Job's distress he begs God for answers. He continually acknowledges the sovereignty of God and is certain that it is God who is afflicting him. His famous words, "Though He slays me yet will I trust him"; reflects Job's love for God that defies comprehension; especially given the fact that he thought that the God that he had given his life to honoring had betrayed him, afflicted him, and sentenced him to shame and defeat.

PRAYER
Dear God,
At times when I feel like you who are sovereign have let me down either because you did not prevent trouble or because I think you actually sent the trouble; help my faith to say sincerely, "thou he slay me, yet will I trust him." You are a good God despite what my circumstances look like.
In the mighty name of Jesus Christ, Amen.

TODAY'S CHALLENGE:

In retrospect, what would it have been like if Job and friends had offered up praise and worship to God instead of engaging in human wisdom and discourse?

What else is God saying to me today?

What is my response?

DAY TWENTY: Job 14-17

Job feels sure of his demise and compares himself to a dry plant that will not be watered and revived. His hope is so crushed that he envies the life of plants that have hope of recovery.

He continues to examine his life and cannot understand the futility of being born, living righteously only to die a miserable death while his friends mock him. He calls his friends miserable comforters; while he contends that he is innocent.

He concedes that his days are over and prepares to die.

PRAYER
Oh God,
you alone are our hope in hopeless situations. At such times help me to shut out the counsel of unwise people and trust in your unfailing love.
In the name of Jesus Christ, I pray Amen.

TODAY'S CHALLENGE:

To avoid anger and disillusionment toward God when I don't understand what is happening in my life?

What else is God saying to me today?

What is my response?

DAY TWENTY-ONE: Job 18-20

Job's friends continue to torment him. He describes Bildad's words as "breaking him into pieces." He describes the utter humility of his situation and begs his friends to have pity on him. Zophar too consents to Job's doom. He tells Job that his blessings did not endure because he is wicked, and that heaven, earth and God has appointed him to wrath.

Job sees no hope for his natural life, but it seems that somewhere from within his spirit, Job makes a prophetic declaration. "I know my redeemer lives, and after my skin is destroyed, this I know, in my flesh I shall see God!"

PRAYER
Oh Lord God Almighty,
when I feel deeply discouraged in my mind and soul, may your Spirit, like an eagle, rise up within me and give me a view of my situation from a loftier perspective. In the name of Jesus Christ, Amen.

TODAY'S CHALLENGE:

Thank God that when my mind and my body resign itself to the grave whether in anguish or in reality, my spirit is still in communion with God.

What else is God saying to me today?

What is my response?

JOURNAL

JOURNAL

INDEX

INDEX

Enjoy - Snow Sledding, Nature walks, Mountain climbing, Watching deer and rabbits, soaring hawks and eagles; nearby Fishing, Camping, Panning for gold, Horse-back riding, Boating and more. It's 20 beautiful acres, located only an hour and fifteen minutes from down town, Los Angeles, but it's a 'whole new world,' a perfect place to recover and heal or relax and reflect.

VICTORY MOUNTAIN RETREAT AND CENTER FOR EMOTIONAL HEALING

is a division of Victory Enterprises and Ministries,
a non-profit organization, founded in 1995.

Our program provides: Counseling/Therapy, Empowerment & Personal Development, Coaching, Training and Seminars, Retreats and Services for Youth.
It is also the future headquarters for the PRAYER THERAPY TRAINING INSTITUTE: (P.T.T.I.).

YOUR SUPPORT IS NEEDED
We are currently seeking Donors, Supporters, Private Investors and Developers to assist us in completing this great work! Please call: 818.771.5525.
Email: drminnie@drminniecounseling.com

www.ingramcontent.com/pod-product-compliance
Lightning Source LLC
Chambersburg PA
CBHW021112080526
44587CB00010B/486